# The Key to the Apocalypse

By Steven Speray

Satan's Final Assault on the Church of Christ

The Apostasy, the Antichrist, and the Abomination

Revealed

Cover design and format by Steven Speray

The Key to the Apocalypse

Copyright 2009 by Steven Speray

ISBN: 978-0-578-04799-7

Published by Confiteor
P.O. Box 83
Versailles, KY 40383
www.catholictopgun.com

# VERITAS

## DEFENDING THE UNDERGR0UND CATHOLIC CHURCH
## 2009

Dedicated to Our Lord, Our Lady, St. Michael,
St. Stephen, St. Patrick,
My Guardian Angel,
and all of Heaven.

O Come, Holy Ghost!

When the Blessed Virgin Mary appeared to Juan Diego in 1531, in the Aztec language, she called herself, *"Te Coatlaxopeuh,"* meaning *"She who crushes the head of the stone serpent."* (Gen. 3:15)

In the end, the Immaculate Heart of Mary will Triumph and it happens with the Second Coming of our Lord Jesus.

# Table of Contents

- Introduction..................................................11
- The Last Days...............................................15
- The Rapture Heresy.......................................19
- The Thousand-Year Reign Fallacy....................25
- The Three Days of Darkness Myth..................29
- The Two Witnesses.........................................33
- The Restoration of Israel................................41
- The Apostasy.................................................49
- How the Church Understands Truth from Apostasy.................53
- Historic Apostasies........................................57
- The Tower of Babel and Freemasonry..............59
- The Infiltration of Communists......................73
- The Apostasy of Today...................................77
- The Antichrist.............................................109
- The Beasts of the Apocalypse........................113
- The Abomination.........................................135
- The Abominations between Antiochus and Paul VI.................141
- The New Mass of Paul VI..............................145

-What makes the New Mass the Abomination........................149

-The Signs of the Times......................................................165

-Birds Eye View of the Apocalypse.........................................167

-The Key..............................................................................169

-Appendix I   Catholic Prophecies about the Apostasy.............171

-Appendix II   The Third Secret of Fatima.............................185

-Index of the Biblical Citations.............................................195


-All Scripture quotes come from one of the following sources:
    -Douay-Rheims (Haydock)
    -Revised Standard Version Catholic Edition

-All papal or saint quotes come from one of the following sources unless otherwise noted:

   -*The Sources of Catholic Dogma*, Denzinger *"Enchiridion Symbolorum,"* Roy J. Deferrari, 13th Edition, Loreto Publications

   -*Decrees of the Ecumenical Councils*, Norman P. Tanner SJ, Sheed & Ward and Georgetown University Press, 1990, Vol. 1 and 2, Tanner

   -*The Faith of the Early Fathers*, William A. Jurgens, Collegeville, MN, The Liturgical Press, 1970, Vol. 1, 2, and 3,

# Introduction

Perhaps the most fascinating religious subject today is eschatology (the study of the last things). Indeed, the subject has been the main focus of the past as well.

Everybody wants to know when and how the end of time will occur. Even the Apostles' asked Jesus, *"Tell us, when shall these things be? And what shall be the sign of thy coming, and of the consummation of the world?"*(Matt. 24:3)

Eschatology begins with Holy Scripture and then with history.

The Holy Scriptures have given us a list of things, signs if you will, that must happen before the Second Coming of our Lord Jesus Christ.

Certain things are givens for each of us, such as death, judgment, heaven and hell. Christians are to meditate on these daily.

However, there are other givens or signs concerning the end of the world as we know it, such as: the Gospel will first be preached throughout the whole world (Matt. 24:14, Mark 13:10), a great apostasy and the antichrist, the man of sin and son of perdition will rise (II Thess. 2:3), and the Second Coming of Jesus (Matt 24:30, Mark 13:26, Colossians 3:4, II Thess. 2:8, I Timothy 6:14, II Timothy 1:10, 4:1,8, Titus 2:13, Hebrews 9:28, I John 2:28, 3:2, Apocalypse 19:7-16, 20:11-13).

Other details are given such as: the conversion and restoration of all Israel, two witnesses who will be martyred, great earthquakes, and in various places famines and pestilences; and there will be terrors and great signs in sun and moon and stars, and upon the earth distress of nations in perplexity at the roaring of the sea and the waves, and then will appear the sign of the Son of man in heaven, and then all the tribes of the earth will mourn, etc.

How all this will unfold is another story.

This study will provide the keys to unlocking the mystery of the Apocalypse so rich in symbolism, thus overcoming the myths and misconceptions of the last days.

The Church Fathers speak extensively on the subject but all disagree on how and when these events will transpire. There were major contentions between them on the details.

The Church has never defined how it will all play out precisely.

The only time the Church gives any real credence to the Fathers is when they all agree on a particular doctrine. As a matter of fact, when they are unanimous, it most likely means that doctrine belongs to the Deposit of Faith.

The Deposit of Faith must be held by all Christians because it comes straight from God, either from Christ, or the Holy Ghost through both the written and oral traditions (II Thess. 2:15).

However, when the Fathers disagree on a topic such as eschatology, their opinions are only that, mere opinions. It is certainly possible for one or more to be heretical. Of course, it would only make those particular Fathers material heretics and not formal ones since none of them were outright contradicting Church doctrine.

A formal heretic knowingly denies true doctrine as opposed to a material heretic which is not a true heretic at all but rather a Christian in mere error. This study will be referring to the former rather than the latter.

The Catechism of the Council of Trent has only one paragraph concerning this aspect of eschatology.

On page 84, the Catechism states, *"the Holy Scriptures inform us that the general judgment will be preceded by these three principal signs: the preaching of the Gospel throughout the world, a falling away from the faith, and the coming of Antichrist."*

Interestingly, there is a little tradition in the Church that when all the fallen angels' places in Heaven will be filled by God's elect, Christ shall come again.

When I sat down to write this book, my intention was to give a broad picture of the Apocalypse in relation to today. The commentary from Rev. George Leo Haydock was going to be my sole source with a little insight from *"The Book of Destiny"* by Rev. Herman Bernard Kramer.

However, many parts of their commentaries didn't add up or completely ignored the important aspects of the Biblical prophecies.

Therefore, I began to do my own little commentaries.

With a world already consumed with Catholicism, I turned all my attention to apocalyptic writing and its symbolism. Each day as I drove at work, going through the Bible in my head, I jotted down thoughts that would be typed out late at night.

About a week or so into the project while drinking a wheat beer at about 3 am (Satan's hour) all the prophecies came together pointing me in the direction of antichrist's identity.

Over ten years ago, the same answer had occurred to me. In trusting in false authorities, I dispelled the thought as incorrect. However, I could not overcome the Bible verses and my conscience. When I tested my theory with the writings of St. John, my suspicions were confirmed.

The answer is so simple and yet the deception of antichrist will continue to lead astray the ones who know his identity.

However, important distinctions must be made with all the different nuances involved.

I don't claim to be infallible and therefore don't claim my work to be without error. If any part is contrary to the Faith, I humbly submit to the Church.

I realize that the following synopsis will come as a surprise to some.

As always with my writings, this work will be completely raw and unedited, although, I have tweaked it as much as possible.

## The Last Days

When the Holy Bible speaks of the last days, it is not referring to the last generation of time but rather from the time of Christ until the end of time or *the* last day.

St. Peter said of the immediate past events of Christ's life and death:

*"But this is that which was spoken of by the prophet, Joel;*
*And it shall come to pass in the last days (saith the Lord) I will pour out of my Spirit upon all flesh and your sons and your daughters shall prophesy, and your young men shall see visions, and your old men shall dream dreams.*
*And upon my servants indeed, and upon my handmaids, will I pour out in those days of my Spirit and they shall prophesy:*
*And I will show wonders in the heaven above and signs on the earth beneath: blood and fire, and vapor of smoke.*
*The sun shall be turned into darkness, and the moon into blood, before the great and manifest day of the Lord cometh.*
*And it shall come to pass, that whosoever shall call upon the name of the Lord, shall be saved.*
*Ye men of Israel, hear these words: Jesus, of Nazareth, a man approved of God among you, by miracles and wonders, and signs, which God did by him in the midst of you. "*(Acts 2:16-22)

Notice that the prophet Joel and St. Peter uses apocalyptic language to describe the First Coming of Christ.

Joseph had visions and dreams, the Star of Bethlehem was a wonder in the heavens, Simeon and Anna prophesied, and hell pursued and ultimately assaulted Jesus.

During His Crucifixion, the sun was darkened which would make the moon appear as blood.

Thus we have a reasonable explanation to the mysterious apocalyptic language.

St. Paul exhorts Timothy to beware of the times of stress in the last days where men will be wicked. But these last days were the present time for Paul and Timothy, not some distant future. (II Tim 3)

When warning the Jewish Christians to be steadfast in the faith, St. Paul actually begins his letter to the Hebrews, *"but in these last days he has spoken to us by a Son, whom he appointed the heir of all things, through whom also he created the world."* (Heb. 1)

In his Epistle, St. Peter preaches, *"Knowing this first, that in the last days there shall come scoffers with deceit, walking according to their own lusts,*
*Saying: Where is his promise, or his coming? For, since the fathers slept, all things continue so from the beginning of the creation.*
*For this they are willfully ignorant of, that the heavens were before, and the earth, out of water and through water, consisting by the word of God:*
*Whereby the world that then was, being overflowed with water, perished.*
*But the heavens which now are, and the earth, by the same word are kept in store, reserved for fire unto the day of judgment, and of the perdition of wicked men.*
*But be not ignorant, my beloved, of this one thing, that one day with the Lord is as a thousand years and a thousand years as one day."* (II Peter 3:3-8)

St. Peter was referring to the last days as the present until the Day of Judgment, which is why he describes the delay. If Peter meant some far off time in the future then this explanation is superfluous.

St. John says, *"Little children, it is the last hour: and as you have heard that antichrist is coming, and now there are many antichrists: therefore we know that it is the last hour."* (I John 2:18)

Therefore, the Holy Bible does not refer to the last days applying only to the last generation but rather to all generations from the time of Christ until the end of time.

The last book in the Holy Bible is the vision of the Beloved Disciple St. John. His vision of the Apocalypse is God's vision as well. St. John is the conduit by which God transmits His vision.

God sees all things at once past, present and future. This is a very important key in unlocking the mystery of the Apocalypse.

The great fallacy in interpreting the Apocalypse is the attempt to confine and constrain all the details and events to fit into the last generation of time.

St. John's Apocalypse should be read with the analogy of faith and interpreted in light of the other Scriptures such as (Matthew 24, II Thessalonians 2, and I John 2) as apocalyptic language can easily be misconstrued, misconceived, and misinterpreted.

This study will not advocate either partial or full preterism since both positions have errors.

Partial preterism is the position that the last days refer to the last days of the Mosaic Covenant, and the destruction of the temple in 70 AD fulfilling the Day of Judgment and Coming of the Lord. It also consists of the belief that the *"Great Harlot"* of the Apocalypse is Jerusalem.

Full preterism is the position that all prophecy was fulfilled with the 70 AD destruction of the temple. This position consists of the belief that the Resurrection of the Dead is not about bodies at the end of time but merely the resurrection of those souls in hell (place of the dead) before Christ.

Both positions misinterpret Christ's words, *"Amen I say to you, that this generation shall not pass, till all these things be done."* (Matt. 24:34)

*"This generation"* refers the generation that will experience the events Jesus just described, not necessarily the present generation of Christ and the Apostles.

St. John tells the Church that it would not be in their day.

# The Rapture Heresy

The Rapture heresy first appeared in the 1800's from John Nelson Darby (Scottish Dispensationalist) and transferred by CI Scofield into his *"Scofield Reference Bible."* It was unheard of prior to the 1800's.

Bible verses such as (I Thess. 4:13-17) are referenced in promoting this heresy. The Rapture is the belief that the Church will be taken up with God in the sky before antichrist and the Great Tribulation and before a thousand-year reign of Christ on earth known as the pre-millennial view, millenarianism or Chiliasm.

The verses from (II Thess. 2:7-8) are referenced in order to show why the Rapture happens before the Tribulation.

Some Rapturists hold that the one who restrains is the Holy Spirit and since the church cannot be without the Holy Spirit then the Rapture happens with the removal of the restraining one. Some simply hold the Church is doing the restraining.

They all reason that we will not be around for the Tribulation because the Bible doesn't explain how we should go through it.

There are other passages that seem to illustrate a pre-tribulational Rapture. (Matt. 24:40-41) states, *"Two men will be out in the field, one will be taken, and one will be left."*

(Luke 17:34-35) gives this account, *"I tell you, on that night there will be two people in one bed: one will be taken, the other left."*

(I Thess. 4:13-17) has it best stating, *"For the Lord himself, with a word of command, with the voice of an archangel and with the trumpet of God, will come down from heaven, and the dead in*

*Christ will rise first. Then we who are alive, who are left, will be caught up together with them in the clouds to meet the Lord in the air. Thus we shall always be with the Lord."* ('Will be caught up' is Rapiemur in Latin, which we get the word 'Rapture.')

This apocalyptic writing can also be found in the books of Daniel and the Apocalypse (Revelation). However, this literary genre common among the ancient Semites should be understood correctly. It is filled with strange illusions, bizarre images with numbers having symbolic meaning.

There are other genres used in Scripture such as the parable, the allegory, and the historical novel. In each literary form, the writer presents but not necessarily asserts the message of God. It is what the writer meant to assert that must be extrapolated. With this in mind, Holy Scripture should be read in the analogy of faith within the historic context and living Tradition of the Church.

If this is not done, then the interpretations will vary with every whim and best guess of the reader and will ultimately end with denying the very Word of God. Scripture itself warns of traditions of men that will nullify the Word of God.

It is interesting to note that immediately after the paragraph used to proof text the Rapture heresy, is found the very Scriptures that tell us about Sacred Tradition. *"Therefore, brothers, stand firm and hold fast to the traditions that you were taught, either by an oral statement or by a letter of ours."* (II Thess. 2:15)

St. Peter warns, *"Know this first of all, that there is no prophecy of Scripture that is a matter of personal interpretation"* (II Peter 1:20) and *"In them there are some things hard to understand that the unlearned and unstable distort to their own destruction, just as they do the other scriptures."* (II Peter 3:16)

Though many saints have preached a literal thousand-year reign of Christ on earth, a pre-tribulational Rapture is novel and since has become an American phenomenon.

The problems with the Rapture heresy:

In the foundation verse for the Rapture (I Thess. 4:15-17), we see that this Rapture happens with the coming of the Lord, *"for we who are alive, who are left until the coming of the Lord, ... Then we who are alive, who are left, will be caught up."*

In (Matthew 24:29-31) and (Mark 13:24-27), when Christ comes again it is immediately after the Great Tribulation. The Rapturist must conclude two second-comings of Christ to keep from contradicting these two passages, and particularly (II Thess. 2:7-8).

Some Rapturists deny two second-comings by reasoning that the Rapture happens when the Lord appears in the sky but doesn't actually make His Second Coming.

Since (I Thess 4) is used to prove this position, the very passage that says the *"coming of the Lord"* wouldn't actually mean the coming of the Lord because He must come later.

Also, the appearance of the Lord in the sky is precisely how Holy Scripture describes the Second Coming. See (Acts 1:11).

The fact is the heretic must believe in two second-comings regardless what they call it. Two second-comings is not the historical Christian belief.

Those verses that speak of being *"caught up"* are simply speaking about the resurrection of the body for all men on the last day. It is a Christian dogma. As a matter of fact, on that same day the damned will find them being *"caught down"* in the same manner.

In (John 11:24), Martha says to Jesus about the death of her brother Lazarus, that she knows that he will be resurrected on the last day. This is what *"caught up"* means in (I Thess. 4).

As for (Matt. 24:40), *"One will be taken; and one will be left,"* simply means that one will be taken to heaven and the other will be left for hell. Look at this verse in light of the next chapter where Christ said He would separate the sheep from the goats. The sheep (Faithful) will be taken and caught up with their bodies, and the goats (unfaithful) will be left and taken down to hell in their bodies. This is the plain explanation of those passages.

In (II Thess. 2:7), the restraining one might be referring to St. Michael but whoever it is, it most certainly is an angel as will be explained later. There is absolutely no reason to believe it is the Church, unless of course you're trying to make it fit into a new theology. It is not so far-fetched to believe that the Holy Spirit is removed or leaves insofar that He will no longer restrains the spirit of antichrist but not leave the Church remnant.

St. Matthew states quite emphatically that the Faithful might have to suffer greatly as it goes through the Great Tribulation. (Matt. 10:22, 24:13)

(Hebrews 11:32-40, 12:1-13) is clearly saying that the Faithful may and will have to suffer greatly.

St. Peter, who holds the primacy in the hierarchy, in (I Peter 1:3-9, 2:18-25, 3:13-17, 4:1) speaks about suffering while our Lord in (Matt. 10:16-18) warns us of the coming persecutions.

The Rapture believing preachers are the very false teachers St. Peter warns us against. (II Peter 2:1)

As for the Rapture, it's simply a false doctrine as understood by the modern heretics.

The focus should be on the Second Coming of the Lord not thinking about getting out of here before the Great Tribulation for we are now going through it.

True Christians hold fast to Sacred Scripture and Sacred Tradition, and profess in the Apostles' Creed, *"He will come again to judge the living and the dead."* On that day, the same Apostles' Creed continues with *"I believe in... the resurrection of the body."*

The resurrection of the bodies to the souls of the Faithful is the true meaning of being *"caught up"* and it happens on the last day of time as we know it when we will enter the age of ages.

As for the Second Coming of our Lord, we will be judged as we live since that day will usher in the Final and General Judgment.

# The Thousand-Year Reign Fallacy

Many of the early Church Fathers held to the belief of Chiliasm also known as the pre-millennial view or millenarianism. This belief holds that Christ will reign on earth for a literal thousand years after the destruction of antichrist.

All the arguments in support of this belief contradicted other passages in Holy Scripture while missing the simple understanding of the literary genre of the Apocalypse.

For instance, the number seven represents completeness or wholeness and is erroneous to believe that seven years must be a literal seven rather than a complete and whole time of trial. The number thousand for the years also represents a round number of a long period of time. It is not to be taken as a literal thousand years.

One could argue that thousand years is a single day since Scripture also has it those thousand years is as one day to the Lord. (II Peter 3:8)

The point is there is another and more proper way to view the thousand years of peace rather than the pre-millennialists, millenarianists, or Chiliasts. On July 21, 1944, Pope Pius XII declared this position couldn't be safely held which is obvious, since one can't logically fit the other events in without contradicting one's self. It's astounding that it took the Church 2000 years to say so.

The Amillennial-view is the understanding that peace comes with the knowledge and unity of Christ. The thousand-year reign of peace began with Jesus who gives peace to his followers. Remember that in apocalyptic language a thousand years represents a round number for a long period of time, and not necessarily a literal thousand years.

Jesus said, *"Peace I leave with you; my peace I give to you; not as the world gives do I give to you. Let not your hearts be troubled, neither let them be afraid."* (John 14:27)

Then Christ repeats Himself:

*"I have said this to you, that in me you may have peace. In the world you have tribulation; but be of good cheer, I have overcome the world."* (John 16:33)

The world has already been defeated by the First Coming of Jesus and peace begins with the Church of Christ which is the household of the faith, the household of God. (Galatians 6:10, Ephesians 2:19, I Peter 4:17)

Therefore, when the thousand years is mentioned in (Apocalypse 20:5-6,) it is clearly referencing the present state of the Church, the household of God.

Satan has no power over the Faithful until he is unleashed for one final assault on the Church. (Apocalypse 20:7)

Just as Christ suffered, died, and was buried, so too, the Church which is His Body (because She is His Bride) must mystically undergo a suffering, death, and burial only to be resurrected on the last day just as the Body of Christ was Resurrected.

St. John explains how the end will appear.

*"And I saw a new heaven and a new earth. For the first heaven and the first earth was gone, and the sea is now no more.*
*And I John saw the holy city, the new Jerusalem, coming down out of heaven from God, prepared as a bride adorned for her husband."* (Apocalypse 21:1-2)

The new heaven and a new earth is an expression of Heaven itself. It will be completely unlike the world we live in that will ultimately pass away. The New Jerusalem is the Church since She is the "*bride*" of Christ (who is the *"husband"*).

*"For this reason a man shall leave his father and mother and be joined to his wife, and the two shall become one flesh." This mystery is a profound one, and I am saying that it refers to Christ and the church."* (Eph. 5:31-32)

## The Three Days of Darkness Myth

Several saints and mystics have prophesied a three days of darkness such as: Anna-Maria Taigi, Padre Pio, St. Hildegard, and Marie-Julie Jahenny, just to name a few.

The prophecy is about a chastisement at the end of the world and can be summed up by the following:

[The world will literally be in darkness for three days during which Devils will be let loose on earth who will kill three quarters of the world's population.
　The Faithful are to lock all the doors and windows not letting anyone in when it happens. Devils will imitate loved ones to fool the Faithful to open up, only then, destroying all those inside. Looking out the window to see the event will cause one to die immediately.
　Rain of fire will fall to earth destroying everything. Only blessed wax candles will give light during those three days and nothing will extinguish them. They won't burn in the houses of the wicked. Because the terror, children will be taken up to Heaven. The Faithful who get caught outside will perish but will be saved from hell. All the enemies of the Church will be annihilated.
　The Faithful are to pray unceasingly during the event.
　After the three days of darkness, those that survive will search far and wide for others who also survived. The earth will be renewed. Sts. Peter and Paul will come down from Heaven and designate a new pope. Christianity will spread and nations will come back to the Church.]

Advocates to this story use bible verses to defend this prophecy. Since a three days of darkness event was seen before in history, such as one of the plagues of Moses, it is seen as a probability rather than a mere possibility.

Because so many mystics and saints have prophesied a future event agreeing on almost every detail, then it is said by those advocates of the prophecy that it would be foolish not to believe that the event will occur.

**The problems with this prophetic scenario in a nutshell**

The first problem is that we see Sts. Peter and Paul likened as the two witnesses of the Apocalypse. Many other prophets and prophesies have spoken about a second-coming of Sts. Peter and Paul to restore Rome. Who would doubt that this was in the minds of those addressing a literal three days of darkness? After all, you have to get those two witnesses in there somehow.

Secondly, this whole scenario simply contradicts itself.

Why would Christianity need to spread if everybody who survives is Christian anyway?

Since only blessed candles can be lit then how do you light your candle unless it is lit before the event takes place?

Such an event is not remotely described in Scripture but rather contradicts it since it leaves no room for the great apostasy, antichrist, and the abomination that happens immediately before the Second Coming. Not to mention that if God destroys all the wicked, then there will be no real separation of lambs and goats during Christ's Judgment.

All such verses used by those who promote the prophecy have been understood outside the genre of apocalyptic language.

If one is looking for a literal three days to happen, then one will not be looking for the antichrist and the Second Coming now!

Padre Pio, just to give one example, has been in error about many things before. For example: he affirmed Garabandal, which had the prophecy that John Paul II would be the last pope of

Catholic times. This means Padre Pio was very wrong about a false apparition since Garabandal has now proven to be untrue as John Paul II was not the last *"pope"* of Catholic times according to the visionaries. However, the times are no different now than when John Paul claimed (falsely) the papacy in 1978.

Padre Pio also believed the book by Maria Valorta *"The Poem of the Man God"* was a good and holy book. However, it was on the index of forbidden books for some heretical statements within it.

There are many prophecies from many saints that never came to pass. Because so many mystics and saints give a prophecy about something alike don't necessarily give it any credence.

The fact is the three days of darkness is heretical unless understood in some symbolic way.

## The Two Witnesses

One of the happenings listed to appear during the last days are the two witnesses who will ultimately die for the Faith. Those two witnesses have been traditionally understood to be the second coming of Elias (Elijah) and Henoch (Enoch).

The Scriptural basis comes from two sources.

*"Behold, I will send you Eli'jah the prophet before the great and terrible day of the LORD comes.*
*And he will turn the hearts of fathers to their children and the hearts of children to their fathers, lest I come and smite the land with a curse."* (Malachias (Malachi) 4:5-6)

*"1 And there was given me a reed like unto a rod: and it was said to me: Arise, and measure the temple of God, and the altar and them that adore therein.*

*2 But the court, which is without the temple, cast out, and measure it not: because it is given unto the Gentiles, and the holy city they shall tread under foot two and forty months:*

*3 And I will give unto my two witnesses, and they shall prophesy a thousand two hundred sixty days, clothed in sackcloth.*

*4 These are the two olive trees, and the two candlesticks, that stand before the Lord of the earth.*

*5 And if any man will hurt them, fire shall come out of their mouths, and shall devour their enemies. And if any man will hurt them, in this manner must he be slain.*

*6 These have power to shut heaven, that it rain not in the days of their prophecy: and they have power over waters to turn them into blood, and to strike the earth with all plagues as often as they will.*

*7 And when they shall have finished their testimony, the beast, that ascendeth out of the abyss, shall make war against them, and shall overcome them, and kill them.*

*8 And their bodies shall lie in the streets of the great city, which is called spiritually, Sodom and Egypt, where their Lord also was crucified.*

*9 And they of the tribes, and peoples, and tongues, and nations, shall see their bodies for three days and a half: and they shall not suffer their bodies to be laid in sepulchres.*

*10 And they that dwell upon the earth shall rejoice over them, and make merry: and shall send gifts one to another, because these two prophets tormented them that dwelt upon the earth.*

*11 And after three days and a half, the spirit of life from God entered into them. And they stood upon their feet, and great fear fell upon them that saw them.*

*12 And they heard a great voice from heaven, saying to them: Come up hither. And they went up to heaven in a cloud: and their enemies saw them.*

*13 And at that hour there was made a great earthquake, and the tenth part of the city fell: and there were slain in the earthquake names of men seven thousand: and the rest were cast into a fear, and gave glory to the God of heaven.*

*14 The second woe is past: and behold the third woe will come quickly.*

*15 And the seventh angel sounded the trumpet: and there were great voices in heaven, saying: The kingdom of this world is become our Lord's and his Christ's, and he shall reign forever and ever. Amen.*

*16 And the four and twenty ancients, who sit on their seats in the sight of God, fell on their faces and adored God, saying:*

*17 We give thee thanks, O Lord God Almighty, who art, and who wast, and who art to come: because thou hast taken to thee thy great power, and thou hast reigned.*

*18 And the nations were angry, and thy wrath is come, and the time of the dead, that they should be judged, and that thou shouldest render reward to thy servants the prophets and the saints, and to them that fear thy name, little and great, and shouldest destroy them who have corrupted the earth.*

*19 And the temple of God was opened in heaven: and the ark of his testament was seen in his temple, and there were lightnings, and voices, and an earthquake, and great hail."* (Apocalypse 11:1-19)

However, these two Scripture passages don't mention Henoch.

How then does Henoch come into the picture as being one of the two witnesses?

If the Apocalypse is to be interpreted as literally two human beings, then Henoch may not be the best substitute since one of them can turn water into blood which more closely fits Moses. It can be seen with the other witness that it is Elias who stops the rain for 1260 days. (James. 5:17, Luke 4:25)

Since Henoch was taken into heaven (Gen. 5:24; Ecclesiasticus (Sirach) 44:16, 49:14, Heb. 11:3), then it is reasoned he would be the one to come back with Elias. This idea comes from apocryphal or extra-biblical writings with examples given below.

The Revelation of Paul: *"And he said to me: This is Enoch, the witness of the last day."*(Ante-Nicene Fathers, Vol. 8, p. 577)

The History of Joseph the Carpenter: *"And I say to you, O my brethren, that they also, Enoch and Elias, must towards the end of time return into the world and die – in the day, namely, of commotion, of terror, of perplexity, and affliction. For Antichrist will slay four bodies, and will pour out their blood like water, because of the reproach to which they shall expose him, and the ignominy with which they, in their lifetime, shall brand him when they reveal his impiety."*(ANF, Vol. 8, p. 394)

The Gospel of Nicodemus: *"One of them answered, and said: I am Enoch, who was well-pleasing to God, and who was translated hither by Him; and this is Helias the Thesbite; and we are also to live until the end of the world; and then we are to be sent by God to withstand Antichrist, and to be slain by him, and after three days to rise again, and to be snatched up in clouds to meet the Lord."* (Chapter 9, *ANF*, Vol. 8, p. 420)

The apocryphal Revelation of St. John the Theologian states: *"And then I shall send forth Enoch and Elias to convict him; and they shall show him to be a liar and a deceiver; and he shall kill them at the altar, as said the prophet, then shall they offer calves upon thine altar."* (*ANF*, Vol. 8, p. 583.)

### The problem with this understanding

Jesus has told his followers that Elias was John the Baptist.

*"For this is he of whom it is written: Behold I send my angel before thy face, who shall prepare thy way before thee.*
*Amen I say to you, there hath not risen among them that are born of women a greater than John the Baptist: yet he that is the lesser in the kingdom of Heaven is greater than he.*
*And from the days of John the Baptist until now, the kingdom of heaven suffereth violence, and the violent bear it away.*
*For all the prophets and the law prophesied until John:*
*And if you will receive it, he is Elias that is to come.*
*He that hath ears to hear, let him hear."* (Matt. 11:10-15)

Take notice that Christ specifically says that we need to hear this and yet so many Christians down through the years until the very day don't.

Jesus says most emphatically, *"And his disciples asked him, saying: Why then do the Scribes say that Elias must come first?*
*But he answering, said to them: Elias indeed shall come, and restore all things.*
*But I say to you, that Elias is already come, and they knew him not, but have done unto him whatsoever they had a mind. So also the Son of man shall suffer from them.*

*Then the disciples understood that he had spoken to them of John the Baptist."*(Matt, 17:10-13)

Christians down through the ages till today do exactly what the Scribes did. They say that Elias must come first before Christ's Second Coming, and yet they don't know that it was John the Baptist during the First Coming of Jesus.

Also, take notice that John the Baptist as Elias will restore all things. See next chapter - The Restoration of Israel.

The Angel of the Lord declares that John the Baptist is Elias come in the spirit.

*"But the Angel said to him: Fear not, Zachary, for thy prayer is heard: and thy wife, Elizabeth, shall bear thee a son, and thou shalt call his name John;*
*And thou shalt have joy and gladness, and many shall rejoice at his birth.*
*For he shall be great before the Lord: and shall drink no wine, nor strong drink, and he shall be filled with the Holy Ghost, even from his mother's womb:*
*And he shall convert many of the children of Israel to the Lord, their God:*
*And he shall go before him in the spirit and power of Elias: that he may turn the hearts of the fathers to the children, and the incredulous to the wisdom of the just, to prepare for the Lord a perfect people."*(Luke 1:13-17)

The Angel prophesies that John the Baptist will convert many of the children of Israel to Christ. Jesus and the Angel fulfill the other prophecy that Israel will be restored and saved.

What then do we make of the words of the Apocalypse?

Since the Apocalypse is in the mysterious apocalyptic language, it must be understood accordingly. St. John's Vision is looking at the whole gamut of salvation history from several different perspectives.

This being the case, the two witnesses, although resembling Elias, Moses, Enoch, etc are but figures of the types of martyrs throughout Christianity. There is no reason to absolutely hold them as two literal men at the end of time.

For instance, the woman in Apocalypse 12 is often understood as the Blessed Virgin Mary. However, St. John also has in mind Israel both old and new.

Israel makes up the people of God. Through Israel of the Old Covenant comes the Messiah (Christ). Christ gives Israel the New Covenant which becomes the Church. The Church is the Bride of Christ. (Eph. 5) Therefore, the woman is the people of God of the Covenants.

The Blessed Virgin Mary, of course, is the perfect model for the Church but the reading of the Apocalypse is not restricted to this interpretation. Indeed, Our Lady is but a secondary interpretation and perhaps the intended primary interpretation.

Apocalyptic language is all about symbolisms, figures, types, and foreshadowing's and is not necessarily constrained to a time table.

The two witnesses are said to have been killed by antichrist.

St. John prophesied that many antichrists will come and go. (I John 2:18).

King Herod was an antichrist and had John the Baptist (the spirit of Elias) killed which fulfills this testimony. Herod also had St. James the Greater killed. (Acts 12:2)

The high priest Caiaphas was an antichrist who may have been the high priest that played a role in killing St. Stephen.

Roman Emperor Nero was seen as an antichrist putting Sts. Peter, Paul, and Bartholomew to death.

The Apostles' Sts. James the Less and Matthias were martyred under the reign of the Roman Emperor and antichrist Claudius.

Pope St. Clement and St. Ignatius of Antioch were killed under the rule of the Roman Emperor and antichrist Trajan.

Roman Emperor and antichrist Marcus Aurelius reigned when St. John's disciple St. Polycarp and Sts. Epipodius and Alexander, Justin, and Cecilia were martyred.

Roman Emperor and antichrist Commodus, the son of Marcus, put St. Apollonius to death.

Sts. Perpetua and Felicity were put to death under the reign of Roman Emperor and antichrist Caracalla.

Pope St. Fabian including Sts. Christopher, Pope Cornelius and Cyprian, Agatha, and Apollania were all martyred under the Roman Emperor and antichrist Decius.

The Roman Emperor and antichrist Valerian put Pope St. Sixtus II and his companions to death including Bishop Saturninus and Bishop Denis and his companions.

St. Lawrence was burned slowly over a fire under the Roman Emperor and antichrist Gallienus and St. Valentine was martyred under antichrist Roman Emperor Claudius II.

Sts. Sebatian, Agnes, Saturninus and companions, Nereus, Achilleus, and Pancras, Donatian and Rogatian, Marcellinus and Peter, Euplius, Januarius, Cosmas and Damian, and Demetrius all died under the antichrist Roman Emperor Diocletian.

Many more examples of witnesses to the Faith who have been martyred could be given, but these suffice.

Paul the hermit and Antony of the desert both very much resembled Elias and John the Baptist. Both were even fed by a raven.

Although never put to death, they lived lives of extreme asceticism which means they carnally died to the world.

Interestingly enough, they lived during the Arian crisis started by a bishop named Arius who denied the divinity of Christ.

Arius should rightly be called antichrist.

The fact remains that martyrdom of these two witnesses may not be actual martyrs, but rather a representation all the Faithful who die to the world, giving witness to the Gospel as they live in the Faith of Christ.

The two witnesses of the Apocalypse represent all of these saints who are in the spirit of Elias, Moses, and Enoch.

St. John uses the number two to represent the East and West.

The two witnesses will spread the Gospel from one end of the earth to the other.

# The Restoration of Israel

One of the common arguments used by heretics and even traditional Catholics these days to prove that Christ's return is imminent is the establishment of the nation of Israel in 1948 which was created by the authority of the United Nations.

This Zionistic belief comes from the pseudo-doctrine that Israel will be restored and saved immediately before the end of time.

St. Paul's Epistle to the Romans is used to defend this doctrine.

*"20 That is true. They were broken off because of their unbelief, but you stand fast only through faith. So do not become proud, but stand in awe.*
*21 For if God did not spare the natural branches, neither will he spare you.*
*22 Note then the kindness and the severity of God: severity toward those who have fallen, but God's kindness to you, provided you continue in his kindness; otherwise you too will be cut off.*
*23 And even the others, if they do not persist in their unbelief, will be grafted in, for God has the power to graft them in again.*
*24 For if you have been cut from what is by nature a wild olive tree, and grafted, contrary to nature, into a cultivated olive tree, how much more will these natural branches be grafted back into their own olive tree.*
*25 Lest you be wise in your own conceits, I want you to understand this mystery, brethren: a hardening has come upon part of Israel, until the full number of the Gentiles come in,*
*26 and so all Israel will be saved; as it is written, "The Deliverer will come from Zion, he will banish ungodliness from Jacob";*
*27 "and this will be my covenant with them when I take away their sins."*

*28 As regards the gospel they are enemies of God, for your sake; but as regards election they are beloved for the sake of their forefathers."* (Romans 11: 20-29)

### The problems with this understanding

First, if the nation of Israel of 1948 is the fulfillment of the prophecy of the restoration, then a tremendous obstacle must be overcome.

The prophecy is about the salvation of Israel not merely a restoring of some nation that we call Israel. The modern day nation of Israel is mostly atheistic and Zionist.

The restoration prophecy is about a spiritual restoration whereby men are saved. The modern day nation we call Israel is not about the salvation for men, but rather is the antithesis of the prophecy. The nation is lost since it rejects Christ.

Secondly, the paradoxical belief has it that all Israel will be saved after a mass conversion of all the Gentiles.

This leaves no room for the Great Apostasy.

(Romans 9:27) is clear that only a remnant of Israel will be saved and (Roman 11:25) reinforces this teaching.

The pseudo doctrine simply contradicts itself.

Verse 25 in Romans is understood as saying by those who hold to the pseudo doctrine that this Israel will be saved after the fullness of Gentiles convert.

However, there is no time left since that fullness happens right up to the Second Coming.

Notice what the Gentiles are coming into.

It is Israel.

The fact is verse 26 says *"all"* Israel is saved at the time of the Deliverer which would be about the First Coming of Christ not the Second. The *"hardening...part of Israel"* ceases to be the true Israel.

The Church is the New Israel with a New Covenant that takes away their sins.

Twice, St. John confirms the Church as the New Jerusalem.

*"He that shall overcome, I will make him a pillar in the temple of my God; and he shall go out no more; and I will write upon him the name of my God, and the name of the city of my God, the new Jerusalem, which cometh down out of heaven from my God, and my new name."* (Apocalypse 3:12)

*"And I John saw the holy city, the new Jerusalem, coming down out of heaven from God, prepared as a bride adorned for her husband."* (Apocalypse 21:2)

Israel and Jerusalem both reference the Church of the People of God.

Verse 25 states that *"part"* of Israel is hardened and can be grafted back in (verse 24). Since God holds that part of Israel as beloved, He is always giving grace to them to be grafted back in but as of now they are enemies of God (verse 28).

The part of Israel that rejects Christ becomes a counterfeit Israel (modern Judaism) to the true Israel (the Church.)

This confirms the Book of Acts chapter 1:

*"5 for John baptized with water, but before many days you shall be baptized with the Holy Spirit."*
*6 So when they had come together, they asked him, "Lord, will you at this time restore the kingdom to Israel?"*
*7 He said to them, "It is not for you to know times or seasons which the Father has fixed by his own authority.*
*8 But you shall receive power when the Holy Spirit has come upon you; and you shall be my witnesses in Jerusalem and in all Judea and Sama'ria and to the end of the earth."* (Acts 1:5-8)

The kingdom of Israel was restored at Pentecost at the birth of the Church.

The Church is the kingdom of Israel and it has now witnessed to all the ends of the earth which fulfills the prophecy that the Gospel will first be preached throughout the whole world (Matt. 24:14, Mark 13:10).

Again, in (Luke 4:18-21 and Matt. 11:5, 12:18) Jesus quotes (Isaiah 61:1-3) as referring to His First Coming and not to His Second Coming.

After reading Isaiah, Jesus says, *"Today, this scripture has been fulfilled in your hearing."*

The next verses in Isaiah references *"rebuilding the ancient ruins."*

In the Book of Acts, St. Peter quotes from (Isaiah and Amos 9:14) as referring to this rebuilding.

*"14 Simon hath related how God first visited to take of the Gentiles a people to his name.*
*15 And to this agree the words of the prophets, as it is written:*
*16 After these things I will return, and will rebuild the tabernacle of David, which is fallen down; and the ruins thereof I will rebuild, and I will set it up;*

*17 That the residue of men may seek after the Lord, and all nations upon whom my name is invoked, saith the Lord, who doth these things.*
*18 To the Lord was his own work known from the beginning of the world."*(Acts 15:14-18)

The prophet Osee (Hosea) spoke, *"For the children of Israel shall sit many days without king, and without prince, and without sacrifice, and without altar."*(Hos. 3:4)

In the Book of Acts, the First Coming of Jesus and the remission of sins for Israel of (Romans 27) was emphasized, *"But Peter answering, and the apostles, said: We ought to obey God rather than men.*
*The God of our fathers hath raised up Jesus, whom you put to death, hanging him upon a tree.*
*Him hath God exalted with his right hand, to be Prince and Saviour, to give repentance to Israel, and remission of sins.*
*And we are witnesses of these things, and the Holy Ghost, whom God hath given to all that obey him."*(Acts 5:29-31)

The book of (Hebrews 10:16-19) refers to the First Coming of Jesus and the remission of sins. Verse 13:10 refers to that altar used for the sacrifice of Christ to be offered for the remission of sins.

Christ fulfills the Kingship, the sacrifice with an altar for the children of Israel and his Church fulfills the doctrine of the restoration of Israel since it was spiritually restored by Christ.

The final antichrist is betting that men recognize the nation of Israel as the Chosen People rather than the Church.

The fact is the children of Israel before Christ were the Chosen People insofar as they maintained their relationship through the Covenant. Otherwise, they were cut off. (Gen. 17:14, Exod. 12:15-19, 30:33- 38, 31:14, Lev. 7:20-27, 17:4-14, 18:29, 19:8,

20:17-18, 22:3, 23:29, Num. 9:13, 15:30-31, 19:13-20, Psalm 37, Jer. 44:7-11, 51:6, Ez. 21:3-4, Dan. 4:14, 9:26)

In the Old Covenant, circumcision became the way to be united to God's Chosen People.

Christ now establishes a new Covenant which includes all men and not just the Jews. For as circumcision became the way in the old, now Baptism replaces circumcision and becomes the way to enter into the Church, the New Covenant, the New Israel, the Chosen People.

*"For we are the true circumcision, who worship God in spirit, and glory in Christ Jesus, and put no confidence in the flesh."* (Phil. 3:3)

*"In him also you were circumcised with a circumcision made without hands, by putting off the body of flesh in the circumcision of Christ."* (Col. 2:11)

*"We were buried therefore with him by baptism into death, so that as Christ was raised from the dead by the glory of the Father, we too might walk in newness of life."* (Rom. 6:4)

*"Baptism, which corresponds to this, now saves you, not as a removal of dirt from the body but as an appeal to God for a clear conscience, through the resurrection of Jesus Christ."* (I Pet. 3:21)

The establishment of the nation of Israel in 1948 is nothing more than the sign that the New World Order ruled by man is replacing the Old World Order when nations were ruled by God as they recognized Christ as King.

It is a great deception to believe the nation of Israel is still the Chosen People as long as its members reject Christ.

Those of the elect who will eventually convert out of that wicked nation may be called Chosen but not the nation as a whole.

If anything, it more aptly resembles the beast of the Apocalypse as a symbol of the antichrist to come.

Therefore, any thought of a future rebuilding of the Temple of Jerusalem would not be a true Temple of God.

Just as a side note, St. Vincent Ferrer converted over 100,000 Jews to Christianity during the fourteenth and fifteenth centuries. This could account for some of those elect children of Israel that would encompass the *"all"* of Israel that will be saved if viewing it from a continuing process of restoration.

# The Apostasy

Apostasy means falling away, or total desertion of the true doctrine of religion. The word is found once in the New Testament (II Thess. 2:3) and implied in several places.

Apostasy is a sin against the Holy Ghost and remaining in apostasy outrages the Spirit, the author and dispenser of grace.

Apostasy is one of the signs that must come before the Second Coming. Throughout Holy Writ, the Faithful are warned against falling away and to endure till the end.

One of the main warnings found in Holy Writ is that of false prophets and christs. Jesus warned His followers of false prophets who come in sheep's clothing but are ravenous wolves (Matt 7:15), and of blind guides (Matt. 15:4), and of false christs (Matt. 24:4, 24).

St. Paul predicts that after his departure ferocious wolves will enter among them, not sparing the flock while spreading erroneous doctrines (Acts 20:29-31, I Tim. 1:10, II Tim. 2:17, III John 9).

Paul also warns the Gentile Christians against the Judaizers who give false doctrine and to avoid them (Rom. 16:17). He warns the Corinthians that they may fall into another gospel just as Eve was seduced by Satan (II Cor. 11:3), and just like Satan transforming himself into an angel of light, so too, do false apostles with their deceitful works masquerading as true disciples (II Cor. 11:13).

As with the Corinthians, Paul also warns the Galatians not to follow another gospel (Gal. 1:6-9).

He warns the Ephesians not to fall into false doctrines (Eph. 4:14), the Philippians to beware of evil workers (Phil. 3:2, 18), the

Colossians not to let men impose the false philosophy of the carnal minds according to the flesh and contrary to the Spirit (Col. 2:8-18), and the Thessalonians not to be led astray by anyone (II Thess. 2:3).

Paul warns the Christian Jews not to fall into apostasy over and over (Hebrews 3:12, 6:4-8, 10:26-29, 12:24-29, 13:9).

St. Peter devotes an entire chapter on warning the Faithful against false prophets and teachers (II Peter 2:1-22).

St. John warns the Faithful against deceivers who ultimately come from hell (I John 3:7-8, 4:1-3. II John 7-11).

Lastly, St. Jude says that in the last time, mockers will come separating themselves and others from the holy Faith.

Although Jesus and His Apostles give ample warnings, we see next a picture how the end of time will appear.

*"For then there will be great tribulation, such as has not been from the beginning of the world until now, nor will be."* (Matthew 24:21, Mark 13:19)

*"38 For, as in the days before the flood they were eating and drinking, marrying and giving in marriage, even till that day in which Noe entered into the ark,*
*39 And they did not understand until the flood came and swept them all away; even so will be the coming of the Son of Man."* (Matthew 24:38-39)

*"26 And as it came to pass in the days of Noe, even so will it be in the days of the Son of Man.*
*27 They were eating and drinking, they were marrying and giving in marriage, until the day when Noe entered the ark, and the flood came and destroyed them all.*

*28 Likewise, as it came to pass in the days of Lot: they were eating and drinking, they were buying and selling, they were planting and building;*

*29 but on the day that Lot went out from Sodom, it rained fire and brimstone from heaven and destroyed them all.*

*30 In the same wise will it be on the day that the Son of Man is revealed.* "(Luke 17: 26-30)

The great flood of Noe wiped out all but 8 people in the world and only Lot's family survived the destruction of Sodom. The Apostasy will leave only a remnant of the Faithful left on earth when Christ comes again.

*"But yet the Son of man, when he cometh, shall he find, think you, faith on earth?"*(Luke 18:8)

Our Lord clearly implies the Faith will almost be extinguished by the time He comes again. When uniting this statement with those found in (Matthew 24, II Thessalonians 2, and the Apocalypse 17 and 18), we have a clearer picture what Christ was telling his followers. It will be worse than anything ever seen in history.

*"3 Let no man deceive you by any means: for unless there come a revolt [apostasy] first, and the man of sin be revealed, the son of perdition,*

*4 Who opposeth, and is lifted up above all that is called God, or that is worshipped, so that he sitteth in the temple of God, showing himself as if he were God.*

*5 Remember you not, that when I was yet with you, I told you these things?*

*6 And now you know what withholdeth, that he may be revealed in his time.*

*7 For the mystery of iniquity already worketh: only that he who now holdeth, do hold, until he be taken out of the way.*

*8 And then that wicked one shall be revealed, whom the Lord Jesus shall kill with the spirit of his mouth, and shall destroy with the brightness of his coming: him,*

*9 Whose coming is according to the working of Satan, in all power, and signs, and lying wonders,*

*10 And in all seduction of iniquity to them that perish: Because they receive not the love of the truth that they might be saved. Therefore God shall send them the operation of error, to believe a lie.*

*11 That all may be judged, who have not believed the truth, but have consented to iniquity."* (II Thessalonians 2:3-11)

*"3 For there shall be a time when they will not endure sound doctrine, but according to their own desires they will heap to themselves teachers, having itching ears :*

*4 And will turn away indeed their hearing from the truth but will be turned to fables."* (II Timothy 4:3-4)

Keep in mind that the prophet Osee (Hosea) spoke of Israel, *"For the children of Israel shall sit many days without king, and without prince, and without sacrifice, and without altar."* (Hos. 3:4)

Just as it happened with Israel of the Old Covenant, so too, can one read Osee as it relates nearly to the letter to the present apostasy of the Church, the New Israel of the New Covenant.

# How the Church Understands Truth from Apostasy

The First Vatican Council (Vatican 1) stated:

*[The object of faith]. Further, by divine and Catholic faith, all those things must be believed which are contained in the written word of God and in tradition, and those which are proposed by the Church, either in a solemn pronouncement or in her ordinary and universal teaching power, to be believed as divinely revealed.* (Dogmatic Constitution concerning the Catholic Faith, Ch. 3, First Vatican Council, Pope Pius IX - *Denzinger* 1792)

Notice, that all teachings from the supreme and ordinary (not just extraordinary) Magisterial must be believed.

Pope Pius IX stated: *"And, we cannot pass over in silence the boldness of those who "not enduring sound doctrine" [II Tim. 4:3], contend that "without sin and with no loss of Catholic profession, one can withhold assent and obedience to those judgments and decrees of the Apostolic See, whose object is declared to relate to the general good of the Church and its right and discipline, provided it does not touch dogmas of faith or morals." There is no one who does not see and understand clearly and openly how opposed this is to the Catholic dogma of the plenary power divinely bestowed on the Roman Pontiff by Christ the Lord Himself of feeding, ruling, and governing the universal Church."* (Pope Pius IX *Quanta Cura* Dec 8, 1864)

*"You will firmly abide by the true decision of the Holy Roman Church and to this Holy See, which does not permit errors."* (Lateran Council V, Bull *Cum postquam* by Pope Leo X)

Pope Leo XIII, *Satis Cognitum* (# 9), June 29, 1896: *"The practice of the Church has always been the same, as is shown by the unanimous teaching of the Fathers, who were wont to hold as outside Catholic communion, and alien to the Church, whoever would recede in the least degree from any point of doctrine proposed by her authoritative Magisterium."*

This statement confirms Vatican 1 that all teachings must be believed because Pope Leo says *"any point of doctrine"* which includes all those doctrines and its components from the universal Magisterium.

Pope Leo XIII, *Satis Cognitum* (# 9), June 29, 1896: *"...But he who dissents even in one point from divinely revealed truth absolutely rejects all faith, since he thereby refuses to honor God as the supreme truth and the formal motive of faith."*

This is a bold statement, because to reject *"one point"* of divinely revealed truth, which is, as Vatican 1 says, all teachings universal and ordinary and extraordinary magisterial teachings, is to reject *"all faith."*

In other words, to reject one point of doctrine is to literally become apostate.

Apostasy is about having the truth first and then falling away, not about being lost beforehand.

Heathens who have never heard the Gospel are not apostates.

Therefore, when St. Paul speaks to the Thessalonians about a great apostasy, he could only be speaking about a falling away from the true religion.

Since he was speaking about the future, the preterist view is in trouble. Christianity spread up to the 70 AD destruction. It cannot be said of the Jews who never accepted Christianity that they fell away from a future point of the destruction since the Old Covenant ended and the New Covenant was established in Christ.

The sign of apostasy could not be visible if it were to mean that the Jews had to accept Christ.

**Pope St. Pius X**

In his encyclical letter, *Our Apostolic Mandate,* on August 25, 1910, Pope St. Pius X already detected *"a great movement of apostasy being organized in every country for the establishment of a One World Church which will have neither dogmas, nor hierarchy... under the pretext of freedom and human dignity."*

*Pascendi,* (on adversaries of the Church), *"not from without but from within; hence the danger is present almost in the very veins and heart of the Church."*

*E Supremi,* (On the Restoration of All Things in Christ): *"5. When all this is considered there is good reason to fear lest this great perversity may be as it were a foretaste, and perhaps the beginning of those evils which are reserved for the last days; and that there may be already in the world the "Son of Perdition" of whom the Apostle speaks (II. Thess. ii., 3). Such, in truth, is the audacity and the wrath employed everywhere in persecuting religion, in combating the dogmas of the faith, in brazen effort to uproot and destroy all relations between man and the Divinity! While, on the other hand, and this according to the same apostle is the distinguishing mark of Antichrist, man has with infinite temerity put himself in the place of God, raising himself above all that is called God; in such wise that although he cannot utterly extinguish in himself all knowledge of God, he has contemned God's majesty and, as it were, made of the universe a temple wherein he himself is to be adored. "He sitteth in the temple of God, showing himself as if he were God"*(II. Thess. Ii., 2).

# Historic Apostasies

Apostasy is the end result of every heresy.

The very first apostasy in Anno Domini is that of the Jews. The Hebrew religion of the Old Covenant was the true religion and the Jews were to accept Christ and His New Covenant to maintain their fellowship as the people of God. Those Jews that rejected Christ fell into apostasy since they had the true faith and lost it. However, this was the present and not the future for the writers of the New Testament.

Other apostasies that came out of the First Century include the Judiazers, Eboinites, Simonians, Cerinthians, and Gnosticism. The Basildians, Carpocratians, Valentinians, Marcionites, Cerdonians, Docetism, Montanists, Encratites, Severians, and Monarchians came out of the Second Century.

Each century following produced its own apostasies. They may have appeared to be great in their day.

The Arian heresy virtually wiped out the Church in the Fourth Century. Arian bishops possessed 97% of the sees.

During the Arian crisis, St. Athanasius stated, *"Even if Catholics faithful to tradition are reduced to a handful, they are the ones who are the true Church of Jesus Christ."* (*Coll. Selecta SS. Eccl. Patrum. Caillu and Guillou*, Vol. 32, pp. 411-412)

Protestantism of the Sixteenth Century was a great apostasy from the true Christian Faith.

Much of Germany, as well as Scandinavia, fell into the apostasy of Lutheranism.

All of England fell into the apostasy of Anglicanism.

Scotland had fallen prey to the apostasy of Calvinism with the Presbyterians.

Arianism and Protestantism were great apostasies and yet Christ has yet to return.

It would appear that the apostasy will be even greater. If nearly the whole world fell in the Arian heresy, and an entire country fell into the Anglican heresy with a million others in Europe, and these are not the great apostasy prophesied in Scripture, how much worse could it be?

Well, it could get a lot worse and indeed it has.

If one country could so easily fall because of a corrupt king and continue through the succession of kings and queens, why not the whole world if deceived by several antipopes?

Modernists argue from the standpoint that the Gates of Hell will not prevail against Rome and therefore reject the idea of Rome losing the Faith. But Christ didn't say Rome but the Church. Rome is only one part of the Catholic Church just as England, Germany, etc.

Rome most certainly can fall away and has fallen away with non-Catholic *"popes"* or antipopes leading the billion-strong flock astray.

It must be a rejection of Catholicism or else it wouldn't be an apostasy at all.

This great falling away corresponds to the definition of apostasy as given by Christ.

With this being said, the subject of the modern day apostasy would be meaningless if modernism or *"the synthesis of all heresies"* is not addressed.

The following pages will address how the modern day apostasy unfolds.

## The Tower of Babel and Freemasonry

The first sin of man is the desire to be like God. All intentional heresies ultimately come from this desire.

*"3 But of the fruit of the tree which is in the midst of paradise, God hath commanded us that we should not eat; and that we should not touch it, lest perhaps we die.*
*4 And the serpent said to the woman: No, you shall not die the death.*
*5 For God doth know that in what day soever you shall eat thereof, your eyes shall be opened: and you shall be as Gods, knowing good and evil.*
*6 And the woman saw that the tree was good to eat, and fair to the eyes, and delightful to behold: and she took of the fruit thereof, and did eat, and gave to her husband who did eat."* (Gen. 3:3-6)

The punishment of attempting to become like God is destruction. God cast man out of paradise and man died both spiritually and physically and the cosmos was forever altered.

The children of Adam and Eve attempted to follow in their parents footsteps trying to achieve where they had failed.

*"3 And each one said to his neighbor: Come let us make brick, and bake them with fire. And they had brick instead of stones, and slime instead of mortar:*
*4 And they said: Come, let us make a city and a tower, the top whereof may reach to heaven; and let us make our name famous before we be scattered abroad into all lands.*
*5 And the Lord came down to see the city and the tower, which the children of Adam were building.*
*6 And he said: Behold, it is one people, and all have one tongue: and they have begun to do this, neither will they leave off from their designs, till they accomplish them in deed."* (Gen. 11:3-5)

The normal way of building is using the simple resources provided by God; stone and mortar. This old world order has men trusting in God for their needs as they live by divine providence.

Eventually, man lost trust and wanted to be independent. They also wanted to be greater, even as great as God. So they made brick and slime to build a tower and a city. The city and tower would represent the unity, power and glory of man for all to see, even God. Man was thumbing his nose at God with his new world order. This new world order of man was destroyed by God since the glory was to be for man evermore.

The Church now represents Christ on earth with the laws of God to keep right order and men holy and upright for salvation.

Some men, antichrists if you will, have always opposed God and Church.

These men realize that their only hope in overcoming the Church on earth is to rebuild the Tower of Babel and a city that replaces Christ's Church.

Rome and its Empire was a great city with the same agenda as those that built the Tower of Babel. It was destroyed as well.

Freemasons are the new builders of the modern New World Order. Hence the name: Masons. Their goal is to build a new society independent of the Church with the god of their choosing. Of course, ultimately that god is themselves. This new society will have men become more technologically advanced not for the glory of God but for man himself.

This New World Order has as a foundation a government ruled by man with laws independent of God's. However, to justify this democratic type of government, the term Christian Republic will be identified as the new form. In other words, Satan rules from the bottom up to the people who make the laws.

The Old World Order has a monarchy or possibly a true Christian Republic where the nation is built upon the laws of God and the Church. In other words, God rules from the top down to the monarchs and then to the people.

The builders of this New World Order are at war with the Catholic Church and at one time both sides were very much aware of this fact.

*"The fight taking place against Catholicism and Freemasonry is a fight to the very death, ceaseless and merciless."* (*Bulletin of the Grand Orient of France*, 1892, p. 183.)

The following substance was discussed in a secret meeting of the Jewish Masonic Lodge of B'nai B'rith in Paris, and reported by the *London Catholic Gazette* of February 1936.

First, a statement concerning B'nai B'rith (Jewish Freemasonry) is needed. Fr. Denis Fahey, in his preface to the "new and revised edition" of Mgr. Dillon's *The War of Antichrist with the Church and Christian Civilization*, 1885, re-titled as *Grand Orient Freemasonry Unmasked as the Secret Power behind Communism*, Christian Book Club, Palmdale, CA, states:

### *FREEMASONRY AND THE JEWISH NATION*

*"The Jewish connection with modern Freemasonry is an established fact everywhere manifested in its history. The Jewish formulas employed by Freemasonry, the Jewish traditions which run through its ceremonial, point to a Jewish origin, or to the work of Jewish contrivers."*

The discussion...

*"Now then, in order to ensure a pope in the required proportions, we must first of all prepare a generation worthy of*

*the kingdom of which we dream . . . Let the clergy move forward under your banner (the Masonic banner) always believing they are advancing under the banner of the apostolic Keys. Cast your net like Simon Bar Jonas; spread it to the bottom of sacristies, seminaries, and convents . . . You will have finished a revolution dressed in the Pope's triple crown and cape, carrying the cross and the flag, a revolution that will need only a small stimulus to set fire to the four corners of the earth.* "(From April 3, 1844, NUBIUS (Piccolo Tigre), *Secret Instructions on the Conquest of the Church*, in Emmanuel Barbier, Les infiltrations masoniques dans l'Eglise, Paris/Brussels: Desclee de Brouwer, 1901, p. 5.)

*"Our ultimate end is that of Voltaire and the French Revolution-the final destruction of Catholicism, and even in the Christian idea... The task that we are to undertake...may take years, perhaps a century... We do not intend to win the Popes to our cause,... our principles, propagators of our ideas... Now then, to assure ourselves a Pope of the required dimensions, it is a question first of shaping for this Pope a generation worthy of the reign we are dreaming of... "In a hundred years time . . . bishops and priests will think they are marching behind the banner of the keys of Peter when in fact they will be following our flag . . . The reforms will have to be brought about in the name of obedience."* (*The Permanent Instruction of the Alta Vendita, the Masonic plan to infiltrate the Catholic Church*)

The Alta Vendita was the highest lodge of the Carbonari (an Italian secret society). Linked with the Freemasons, the Carbonari was found throughout Europe and operated primarily in Italy and France. The Permanent Instruction was a secret document with the plan to infiltrate the Church all the way to the papacy. Its goal was to change the Faith to the Masonic principles, which is modernism, liberalism, and the religion of man whereby all religions are recognized as legitimate practices pleasing God and all men are united in the one goal of having one secular system of government under this one form of religion.

Popes Pius IX and Leo XIII commanded the Permanent Instruction to be exposed through publication to prevent the plan from taking effect. Popes Pius IX, Leo XIII and St. Pius X all condemned liberalism and modernism as the form found under Masonic principles. Pope St. Pius X was elected in 1903 with Austria vetoing the first election of Cardinal Rampolla, reported to be the Mason implant.

*"If one takes into consideration the immense development which [the]... secret societies have attained; the length of time they are persevering in their vigor; their furious aggressiveness; the tenacity with which their members cling to the association and to the false principles it professes; the persevering mutual cooperation of so many different types of men in the promotion of evil; one can hardly deny that the Supreme Architect of these associations (seeing that the cause must be proportional to the effect) can be none other than he who in the sacred writings is style the Prince of the World; and that Satan himself even by his physical cooperation, directs and inspires at least the leaders of these bodies physically cooperating with them."* ("*Acta Sancta Sedis*", v. 1, p. 293, 13 July 1865, Pope Pius IX)

Pope Leo warned, *"...the Sect's purpose is to reduce to naught the teaching and authority of the Church among the civilian population.... The enmity of the sectarians against the Apostolic See of the Roman Pontiff has increased its intensity... until now the evil doers have reached the aim which had, for a long time that of their evil designs, namely, their proclamation that the moment has come to suppress the Roman Pontiff's sacred power and to completely destroy this Papacy which was divinely instituted."*(*Humanum Genus*, 1884, Pope Leo XIII)

*"The goal is no longer the destruction of the Church but rather to make use of it by infiltrating it."* (*'Ecumenism'* Freemason book, 1908, found in Bishop Graber, St. Athanasius, pp. 64-65)

"A day will come when the pope, inspired by the Holy Spirit will declare that all the excommunications are lifted and all the anathemas are retracted, when all the Christians will be united within the Church, when the Jews and Moslems will be blessed and called back to her . . . she will permit all sects to approach her by degrees and will embrace all mankind in the communion of her love and prayers. Then, Protestants will no longer exist. Against what will they be able to protest? The sovereign pontiff will then be truly king of the religious world, and he will do whatever he wishes with all the nations of the earth." (Notorious Freemason Eliph Levi 1862, found in Dr. Rama Coomaraswamy, *The Destruction of the Christian Tradition*, p. 133)

"Cagliostro was the Agent of the Templars, and therefore wrote to the Free-Masons of London that the time had come to begin the work or re-building the Temple of the Eternal...A lodge inaugurated under the auspices of Rousseau, the fanatic of Geneva, became the center of the revolutionary movement in France... The secret movers of the revolutionary movement in France... The secret movers of the French Revolution had sworn to overturn the Throne and the Altar upon the Tomb of Jacques de Molay. When Louis XVI was executed, half the work was done; and thenceforward the Army of the temple was to direct all its efforts against the Pope." (*Morals and Dogma*, 1871, Albert Pike, pp. 823-824)

In 1878, Masonic Brother and member of the French Parliament, Bethmont boasted to Bishop Pie of Poitiers, "...Violence against the Church leads nowhere; we shall use other means. We shall organize a persecution which shall be both clever and legal; we shall surround the church with a network of laws, decrees and ordinances which will stifle it without shedding one drop of blood." (*Papacy and Freemasonry*, Msgr. Jouin, 1955, pp. 23-24)

"To fight against the Papacy is a social necessity and constitutes the constant duty of Freemasons." (The Report of the Masonic International Congress held in Brussels, in 1904)

*"Let us remember that as long as there still remain active enemies of the Catholic Church, we may hope to become Masters of the World...[nevertheless] the future Jewish King will never reign in the world before the Pope in Rome is dethroned as well as all the other reigning Monarchs of the Gentiles upon earth."* (*Parisian weekly*, Le Revell du Peuple quote, in *The Masonic Plan to Suppress the Papacy as Admitted by the Freemasons Themselves, Exile of the Pope Elect;* Part VIII, Gary Giuffre)

Albert Pike (1809-1891), who was just previously quoted, was a 33$^{rd}$ degree Freemason and one of the founding fathers and head of the Ancient Accepted Scottish Rite of Freemasonry and the Grand Commander of North American Freemasonry.

Pike studied at Harvard and could read and write in 16 different languages. He served as Brigadier-General in the Confederate Army.

President Andrew Johnson dedicated a Masonic Temple in Pike's honor, and it is the only monument of a Confederate general in Washington, D.C.

Albert Pike was also a leader in the Knights of the Ku Klux Klan.

His 1871 book, *"Morals and Dogma of the Ancient and Accepted Rite of Freemasonry"* is one of the great sourcebooks honored in Freemasonry. It is loaded with all sorts of occultism.

Being a Luciferian, Pike wrote: *"Every Masonic lodge is a temple of religion; and its teachings are instruction in religion...Masonry, like all religions, all the Mysteries, Hermeticism and Alchemy, conceals its secrets from all except the Adepts and Sages, or the Elect, and uses false explanations and misinterpretations of its symbols to mislead...to conceal the Truth, which it calls Light, from them, and to draw them away from it... The truth must be kept secret, and the masses need a teaching proportioned to their imperfect reason... every man's conception of God must be proportioned to his mental cultivation, and intellectual powers, and moral excellence. God is, as man conceives him, the reflected image of man himself. The true name of Satan, the Kabalists say, is that of Yahveh reversed: for Satan is not a black god... Lucifer, the Light Bearer! Strange and mysterious name to give to the Spirit of Darkness! Lucifer, the Son of the Morning! Is it he who bears the Light...Doubt it not!"*

Is it any wonder why Catholicism and Freemasonry are opposed?

Yet, the plan of the Masons to infiltrate the Church was finally realized.

*"Within the eight city blocks that make up the Vatican State no fewer than four Scottish Rite lodges are functioning. Many of the highest Vatican officials are Masons and in certain countries where the Church is not allowed to operate, it is the lodges that carry on Vatican affairs, clandestinely."* (In a 1993 interview with the political weekly Processo, Grand Commander of the Supreme Council of Masons of Mexico, Carlos Vazquez Rangel.)

Again, Vazquez, *"On the same day, in Paris the profane Angelo Roncalli and the profane Giovanni Montini were initiated into the august mysteries of the Brotherhood. Thus it was that much that was achieved at the Council was based on Masonic principles."*

In 1958 and 1963, both Roncalli and Montini who were initiated into the Brotherhood together in the late 40's, came out of their respective conclaves as *"Popes"* John XXIII and Paul VI.

Both men fixed all future elections as Paul VI curtailed the age limit of Cardinals to vote and be voted in. Over 80 cardinals were barred from the 1978 conclaves that produced John Paul I and II. The 1978 conclaves was stacked. John had appointed 8 cardinals and Paul had appointed 100 cardinals out of 111 that voted. Since John and Paul were really antipopes due to their affiliation with Masonry, their cardinals would ipso facto be invalid. Only Cardinals Wyszinski, Leger, and Siri who participated were valid cardinals.

As for the name John Paul that was taken by Luciani, *"the special significance of that name can be found in the thick book on Masonic Morals and Dogma, in which only two Saints' names are honored --- John and Paul. According to the doctrine expressed in this book, the Masons pretend that John the Baptist taught an esoteric doctrine of the Essenes; and they favor "Paul" because of his supposed "leniency," what the opponents of the Papacy have made of Paul's apparent opposition to Peter on one point. I have often mentioned Montini's wearing of the emblem of the high priesthood of Royal Arch Masonry, and I have on file a photo of John XXIII wearing a white glove which prominently displays the sun symbol of the Gnostics. By a top French Mason, Yves Maursodon, John XXIII and Paul VI were praised in the foreword of a book on Freemasonic ecumenism. Despite what was quoted from Paul VI in "Counter-Reformation," which I repeated on another page, there is no mystery at all about Montini's ecumenism."* (*Excerpt from W.F. Strojie Letter* No. 21, May 25 1977.)

However, the 1917 Code of Canon Law has an automatic excommunication for those who belong to Masonry. Can 2335 states: *Persons joining associations of the Masonic sect or any others of the same kind which plot against the Church and legitimate civil authorities contract <ipso facto> excommunication simply reserved to the Apostolic See.*

This means Roncalli and Montini were not Catholics. Even if they are only serious suspect of being Masons, they cannot be considered popes since doubtful popes are impossible.

The Vatican 2 Church has not done away with this law. By keeping it, the new religion of Rome cleverly hides the fact that she is in fact Masonic.

Those that reject the testimony of Yves Marsaudon that Roncalli and Montini became Freemasons should take note of the following.

When Roncalli was Papal Nuncio in Paris, he would visit the Grand Lodge of that city in civilian clothes every Thursday evening as testified by several members of the French police appointed to guard him. (This information can be substantiated by Commandant Rouchette, the retired French police at B.P. 151, 18105 Cognac Cedex. France. Also noted in Mary Ball Martinez, The Undermining of the Catholic Church, Hillmac, Mexico, 1999, p. 117.)

While in France, he appointed a thirty-third degree Freemason and close friend, the Baron Yves Marsaudon, as head of the French branch of the Knights of Malta, a Catholic lay order, causing a major scandal for the Pius XII papacy. (Paul I. Murphy and R. Rene Arlington, *La Popessa*, 1983, pp. 332-333)

Yves Marsaudon wrote: *"The sense of universalism that is rampant in Rome these days is very close to our purpose for existence... with all our hearts we support the revolution of John XXIII."* (Yves Marsaudon in his book *Ecumenism Viewed by a Traditional Freemason*, Paris: Ed. Vitiano; quoted by Dr. Rama Coomaraswamy, *The Destruction of the Christian Tradition*, p. 144.)

Is it a mere coincidence that Vatican 2 and the revolution of the Church took place immediately after the 1958 Conclave?

After being elevated to the College of Cardinals, Roncalli even insisted upon receiving the red hat from the notoriously anti-clerical Vincent Auriol, President of the Masonic *"Fourth Republic"* of France.

Again, 33rd Degree Freemason and good friend of John XXIII Marsaudon wrote, *"If there are still some remnants of thought, reminiscent of the Inquisition, they will be drowned in a rising flood of ecumenism and liberalism. One of the most tangible consequences will be the lowering of spiritual barriers that divide the world. With all our hearts we wish for the success of John XXIII's Revolution."* (*L'oecumenisme vu par un Franc Macon de Tradition*, Yves Marsaudon, 1964, Paris, p. 26.)

The dedication and preface for Marsaudon's book was written by Charles Riandley, Sovereign Grand Commander of the Supreme Council of France (Scottish Rite). Riandley wrote: *"To the memory of Angelo Roncalli, ... Pope under the Name of John XXIII, Who Has Deigned to Give Us His Benediction, His Understanding and His Protection, ... [and] To His August Continuer, His Holiness Pope Paul VI."* Riandley confidently predicted how the policies of Roncalli and Montini would advance the Masonic agenda: *"We are convinced of the narrowness of the spiritual, cultural, scientific, social and economic structures which up to our own time, have hindered the actions and the thoughts of man... But these structures have already been shattered in part. Some pontifical decisions have contributed to this. We feel sure that they will be all destroyed eventually... True, not everything is to be rejected; but what cannot be saved will not be saved unless it is renovated."* (*L'oecumenisme vu par un Franc Macon de Tradition*, Yves Marsaudon, 1964, Paris, p. 15, 16.)

The *Masonic Bulletin*, the official organ of the Supreme Council of the 33rd Degree of the Ancient and Accepted Scottish Rite of Masons, for the Masonic District of the United States of Mexico, located at 56 Lucerna St., Mexico, D.F. (Year 18, No. 220, May 1963):

### *"THE LIGHT OF THE GREAT ARCHITECT OF THE UNIVERSE ENLIGHTENS THE VATICAN*

"Generally speaking, the encyclical Pacem in Terris, addressed to all men of goodwill, has inspired comfort and hope. Both in democratic and Communist countries it has been universally praised. Only the Catholic dictatorships have frowned upon it and *distorted its spirit. "To us many concepts and doctrines it contains are familiar. We have heard them from illustrious rationalist, liberal, and socialist brothers. After having carefully weighed the meaning of each word, we might say that, the proverbial and typical Vatican literary rubbish notwithstanding, the encyclical Pacem in Terris is a vigorous statement of Masonic doctrine... we do not hesitate to recommend its thoughtful reading."* (Fr. Joaquin Saenz Y Arriaga, S.J. Fr., *The New Montinian Church*, pp. 147-148.)

Fr. Joaquin also reported in his book:

*"From the June 4, 1963, edition of The Reporter (El Informador):*

*"The Great Western Mexican Lodge of Free and Accepted Masons, on the occasion of the death of John XXIII, makes known its sorrow for the disappearance of this great man who revolutionized the ideas, thoughts, and forms of the Roman Catholic liturgy. His encyclicals Mater et Magistra and Pacem in Terris have revolutionized the concepts favoring human rights and liberty. Mankind has lost a great man, and we Masons acknowledge his high principles, his humanitarianism, and his being a great liberal. Guadalajara, Jal., Mexico, June 3, 1963 Dr. Jose Guadalupe Zuno Hernandez"* (Fr. Joaquin Saenz Y Arriaga, S.J., *The New Montinian Church*, p. 147)

John XXIII was hailed and honored by Masons everywhere admitting that his vision of Christianity was none other than the One World Church Pope St. Pius X warned us about.

*"The direction of our action: Continuation of the Work of John XXIII and all those who have followed him on the way to Templar Universalism."* (*Resurgence du Temple*, published and edited by the Knights Templar (Freemasons), 1975 A.D.O. Datus, *"Ab Initio,"* p. 60.)

Lastly, the great Mexican priest Fr. Joaquin Saenz Y Arriaga wrote about Roncalli's successor Montini and makes a fascinating observation:

*"Now then, the breastpiece was a prominent Jewish emblem. It symbolically represented the twelve tribes of carnel Israel at the ritual celebrations. Nothing, then, justifies the wearing of this ritual object by a Pope, the visible head of the new people of God, the children of the New Covenant. Even the fact that no previous Pope during the 2,000-year history of the Church has ever worn this ritualistic object of religious Judaism, seems to demonstrate that there is an absolute incompatibility between the profession of our Catholic Faith and the wearing of the ephod or "breastplate of judgment," thoroughly described in the Exodus as characteristic and exclusive of the Levitical high priest.*

*Since Paul VI wore it publicly, we have the right, and moreover, a grave obligation of conscience to investigate why...John Baptist Montini wears the breastpiece because in his heart, rather than a Pope, he is a Levitical high priest. Consciously or unconsciously, only God knows, he seems to be associated with international Judaism, its mighty leaders, and its destructive tools of Communism and Masonry. On the other hand, in his genealogical line of ancestors we find actual roots of Jewish origin, just as in the cases of other cardinals, monsignors, and theologians who have masterminded this dreadful revolution in God's Church."* (Fr. Joaquin Saenz Y Arriaga, S.J. PHD., *The New Montinian Church*, 1971 A.D. pp. 302-303)

It has already been shown how Lucifer is part of Freemasonry.

*"XXXVIII: What is more absurd and more impious than to attribute the name of Lucifer to the Devil, that is, to personified evil. The intellectual Lucifer is the spirit of intelligence and love; it is the paraclete [an advocate]; it is the Holy Spirit, where the physical Lucifer is the great angel of universal magnetism."* (Eliphas Levi, *The Mysteries of Magic, A Digest of the Writings of Eliphas Levi*)

Exorcist Fr. Malachi Martin reported that on June 29, 1963, the night before Paul VI's coronation, a black mass was celebrated and Satan was enthroned in the Vatican! *(Windswept House)*

Fr. Malachi has confirmed several times in interviews that this is a fact from his book, and has believed the Vatican has been possessed by Satan ever since.

In an Address to the United Nation General Assembly on Oct. 4, 1965, Paul VI praises the United Nations *"as the last hope of concord and peace."*

He is saying forget about the Church as the last hope of concord and peace. The New World Order is it. In a message to the United Nations on May 24, 1978, Paul VI called for a New World Order. (*L'Osservatore Romano*, June 15, 1978, p. 3.)

## The Infiltration of Communists

Not only is the Church being attacked by secret societies specifically the Freemasons, but also by the Communists.

For years, the Communists have used the same tactic as the Masons; infiltration.

Their goal is to destroy the Church with their new Tower and City of Babel.

*"Dr. Alice von Hildebrand recalled during an interview that "Bella Dodd told my husband and me that when she was an active [Communist] party member, she had dealt with no fewer than four cardinals within the Vatican 'who were working for us'." (Vatican 2 in the Dock,* Jan, 2003, this interview took place 20 years before Vatican 2)

Mrs. Bella Dodd was in the Communist Party of America.

She defected and converted to the Catholic Church in 1952 through Bishop Fulton Sheen.

Dodd testified before the House American Activities Committee that she was personally responsible for planting over 1,000 men in Catholic seminaries in order to destroy the Church from within.

She gave lectures in the 1950's telling how in the 1930's *"we (Communists) put eleven hundred men into the priesthood in order to destroy the Church from within."* She said then that, *"Right now they are in the highest places in the Church"* with changes that will cause you in the future not to recognize the Catholic Church as the Faith would be destroyed and apologizing for the past errors of intolerance while not recognizing other religions.

Manning Johnson, (former Communist official) told the same Committee in 1953 that by *"concentrating Communist agents in the seminaries"* it was intended that *"a small Communist minority [would] influence the ideology of future clergymen in the paths conducive to Communist purposes."* And he added: *"This policy of infiltrating seminaries was successful beyond even our communist expectations."*

In 1944, Montini (later Paul VI) worked with the Soviets through a childhood friend Togliatti, who was head of the communist Party in Italy. The Archbishop Primate of the Protestant Church in Sweden, who was state official, informed Pope Pius XII of the situation. It came as shock to Pius XII who exiled Montini to Milan without the traditional red hat. He was so angry that he refused the cardinal's beretta from Pius XII. Investigations into Montini's Soviet affair resulted in finding that his private secretary, the Jesuit Tondi, was a KGB agent who was once the Professor of Atheism at the University of Maxism-

Leninism. Tondi gave the Soviets the names of all the clergy sent to Russia who were immediately caught and executed. Tondi was imprisoned and later married his mistress, the militant communist Carmen Zanti in a civil service. After Montini's election to the papacy, Tondi returned to Rome to work in the Vatican's Civil Service as a cover for his KGB activities. Paul VI was greeted on the balcony after his *"election"* with cries of *"il Papa Montinovsky."*

Paul VI was simply a communist sympathizer. The Pact of Metz held in 1962, guaranteed that the Vatican would not condemn communism at the Second Vatican Council. However, earlier, in 1942, talks already were in the works with communist Moscow. *"It was in that year, that Vatican Monsignor Giovanni Battista Montini, who himself later succeeded to the Papacy as Paul VI, talked directly with Joseph Stalin's representative. Those talks were aimed at dimming Pius XII's constant fulminations against the Soviet dictator and Marxism. Stato himself had been privy to those talks. He had also been privy to the conversations between Montini and the Italian Communist Party leader, Palmiro Togliatti, in 1944.... "Stato offered to supply reports from the Allied Office of Strategic Services about the matter, beginning, as he recalled, with OSS Report JR-1022 of August 28, 1944"* (Malachi Martin, *The Jesuits - The Society of Jesus and the Betrayal of the Roman Catholic Church*, New York: Simon & Schuster, 1987; pp. 91-92)

Mark Winckler, interpreter working at the Vatican, tells of a meeting he had with Cardinal Pignedoli (then Msgr.) Pignedoli told him in 1944 that the failed Freemasonic plan to have Cardinal Rampolla elected pope in 1903 would be corrected when they elect Montini. (*The Destruction of the Christian Tradition*, updated and revised, 2006, Rama P. Coomaraswamy p. 145.)

As been demonstrated, the kingdom of Satan is unified and not divided through its diverse attacks.

Freemasonry, Communism, and even Islam or Mohammedism may appear to be enemies, but the reality is that they are united against Christianity.

All three ultimately have the same goal.

Today, Muslims have infiltrated the West bringing the laws and customs of the Islamic religion, thus bringing down what little goodness is left.

# The Apostasy of Today

As Pope St. Pius X sadly pointed out, the establishment of a One World Church was being established in his day.

Taken straight out of the playbook of Teilhard de Chardin, Paul VI said, *"Our times, can they also not have an Epiphany which corresponds to its spirit, to its capacities? The marvelous scientific evolution of our days, can it not become this star, this sign that thrusts modern humanity towards a new quest for God, towards a new discovery of Christ?"* (Milan, 1956, *Le Pape de l'Epiphanie*)

Later, he would state, *"Modern man, will he not gradually come to the point where he will discover, as a result of scientific progress, the laws and hidden realities behind the mute face of matter and give ear to the marvelous voice of the spirit that vibrates in it? Will this not be the religion of our day? Einstein himself glimpsed this vision of a universal religion produced spontaneously [i.e., without revelation]. Is this not perhaps today my own religion?"* (Conference in Turin, March 27, 1960)

This new religion, as it were, comes out from under the establishment of the New World Order; the new Tower of Babel.

All governments are ruled by some type of religion, even the atheistic type. Therefore, politics and religion cannot be separated.

The new religion has as its foundation *'that what was true yesterday is not necessarily true today.'* This core belief is known as *modernism*.

Today's great apostasy is modernism since it redefines truth and what is true for the moment. The system holds that not all truth is immutable. In other words, modernism is the belief that doctrine and truth evolves.

Since modernism is the system that holds a doctrine as being true at one point in time and then ceasing to be true at another point in time, the modernist, then, could logically contradict himself throughout time. This *"new truth"* becomes nothing more than a convenient truth for the modernist.

In July 1907, St. Pius X disclosed the document *Lamentabili Sane Exitu*, which comprehensively condemned sixty-five propositions as pertaining to modernism.

Later, in September 1907, St. Pius X promulgated an encyclical *Pascendi dominici gregis* which enjoined a mandatory Oath Against Modernism on all Catholic Clergy and teachers. In it, St. Pius X denounced modernism as the *"synthesis of all heresies"* because this new system of belief allows the interjection of whatever man wants to hold as true.

The oath was abolished by Paul VI in 1967.

In 1990, Joseph Ratzinger aka Benedict XVI stated: *"the declarations of Popes in the last century [19th century] about religious liberty, as well as the anti-Modernist decisions at the beginning of this century, above all, the decisions of the Biblical Commission of the time [on evolutionism]... in the details of the determinations they contain, they became obsolete after having fulfilled their pastoral mission at their proper time."* (Joseph Ratzinger, *"Instruction on the Theologian's Ecclesial Vocation,"* published with the title *" (Rinnovato dialogo fra Magistero e Teologia,"* in *L'Osservatore Romano*, June 27, 1990, p. 6)

This statement by Ratzinger is modernist in itself. For he is saying that the condemnations of the Catholic Church were only pastoral that applied to a certain period of time rather than doctrinal that applied throughout all time. In other words, truth changes with the times.

In fact, the condemnations actually condemn Ratzinger's statement. Read the condemnations from *The Syllabus of Errors* on the following pages.

This all brings us to the One World Church.

The new religion is really the conglomerate of all religions.

If all religions are more or less good with essentially the same social goals, then why not introduce the doctrine that man has a right to publically practice the religion of his choice?

This is precisely what happened.

However, Pope Pius IX and the Church condemned this doctrine in *The Syllabus of Errors* along with many other similar fallacious doctrines.

Examples of the following errors condemned by Pope Pius IX in encyclical, *The Syllabus of Errors*:

> 55. The Church ought to be separated from the State, and the State from the Church. -- Allocution *"Acerbissimum,"* Sept. 27, 1852.
>
> X. ERRORS HAVING REFERENCE TO MODERN LIBERALISM
>
> 77. In the present day it is no longer expedient that the Catholic religion should be held as the only religion of the State, to the exclusion of all other forms of worship. -- Allocution *"Nemo vestrum,"* July 26, 1855.
>
> 78. Hence it has been wisely decided by law, in some Catholic countries, that persons coming to reside therein shall enjoy the public exercise of their own peculiar worship. -- Allocution *"Acerbissimum,"* Sept. 27, 1852.

*79. Moreover, it is false that the civil liberty of every form of worship, and the full power, given to all, of overtly and publicly manifesting any opinions whatsoever and thoughts conduce more easily to corrupt the morals and minds of the people, and to propagate the pest of indifferentism.* -- Allocution *"Nunquam fore,"* Dec. 15, 1856.

*80. The Roman Pontiff can, and ought to, reconcile himself, and come to terms with progress, liberalism and modern civilization.* --Allocution *"Jamdudum cernimus,"* March 18, 1861.

All these condemnations were largely ignored as nations with developed democratic governments kept out the authority of Christ and the Church.

John XXIII also ignored it and wrote a Masonic type of encyclical that was praised by General Secretary of the British Communist Party, John Gollan, before television cameras on April 21, 1963, who said the, *"encyclical (Pacem in Terris) [of John XXIII] had surprised and gladdened"* him and, therefore, he had externalized his *"most sincere satisfaction at the recent 28th Party Congress."* (Fr. Joaquin Saenz Y Arriaga, *The New Montinian Church,* Brea, CA., p. 170.)

John XXIII wrote in *Pacem in terris* #14, April 11, 1963: *"Also among man's rights is that of being able to worship God in accordance with the right dictates of his own conscience, and to profess his religion both in private and in public."*

With the civil law that all men are created equal with the right to be equal in status among men, comes the law that all religions are equal, thus, all religions are treated equally. One religion cannot be superior with all others being inferior or else the modernist man will view those with inferior religions as inferior or second-class citizens.

Equal religions translate over to those who reject Christ, thus, such religions with their false gods are made equal to Christ insofar as the law is enforced.

Nations, such as the United States which was founded on this antichristian principle, become more secular. This only leads Catholics accepting non-Catholics as equal insofar as their particular religion doesn't intrude the freedom to practice their own.

The French Revolution used the American concept of the US Declaration of Independence for its own *Declaration of the Rights of Man and of the Citizen*. This devastating document destroyed the authority of Christ and Church as the model for French law and government.

Once the patriot holds his nation's views that overshadow his Catholic belief as it happened with the Americans and French, the belief that all religions are more or less good becomes solidified.

Patriotism is obligatory, but God first. Remember the famous last words of St. Thomas More to the world uttered as he stood waiting to be executed for treason against England and King Henry VIII, *"I die the King's good servant, but God's first."*

After Pope Pius IX issued *The Syllabus*, Pope Leo XIII promulgated on January 22, 1899 (on the insistence of devout Catholics such Bishop Corrigan of New York) the encyclical *Testem Benevolentiae Nostrae* condemning Americanism as a heresy.

The encyclical outlines how widespread Americanism is by stating, *"To put an end to certain contentions which have arisen lately among you, and which disturb the minds, if not all, at least of many."*

Then Pope Leo sums up the problem stating, *"For it would give rise to the suspicion that there are among you some who conceive and would have the Church in America to be different from what it is in the rest of the world."*

When Cardinal Gibbons received this encyclical from the pope, he hid it from the Catholics in America until he was exposed. He was clearly one of those Americanists whom the pope was condemning in the encyclical.

In his book "*The Faith of Our Fathers,*" Gibbons promotes religious liberty as the right of man failing to make the correct distinctions between coercion, rights, and tolerance.

As Solange Hertz so rightly points out in, *"The Star-Spangled Heresy: Americanism,"* "*Although he [Gibbons] denied the heresy in word, there is no getting around the fact that he lived it in deed, his whole life illustrating the false principle Leo condemned: "that, in order the more easily to bring over to Catholic doctrine those who dissent from it, the Church ought to adapt herself somewhat to our advanced civilization, and relaxing her ancient rigor, show some indulgence to modern popular theories, and methods, even to pass over certain heads of doctrines, as if of lesser moment, or to soften them that they may not have the same meaning which the Church has invariably held."*

Pope St Pius X said in his *letter to Sillon,* *"The state cannot be built unless the Church lays the foundations and supervises the work."* The USA was built by men wanting independence from God and the Old World Order which is the Catholic State. Men would now rule deciding what is right and wrong apart from the Church and Divine Revelation. All religions would be recognized as legitimate which the Catholic Church has repeatedly condemned.

The New World Order as it says on the one dollar bill has now replaced the Old World Order. Democracy has taken over every Catholic State in the world with wars being fought in order to establish more democracies around the globe until the whole world is one great big democracy. Islamic countries are the last contenders and they are even falling into the trap under what they call Sharia Law.

Pope Leo XIII in *Graves communi* and Pope St Pius X in *Notre Charge Apostolique* solemnly teach that God's authority does not come from the people, yet the US government is ruled by the people with an unauthorized authority since God never authorized it. Governments are to be run through a hierarchy. Democracies, such as the US, are simply anti-Catholic in nature.

The American *"Catholic"* hierarchy would have us believe that you can hold both and the majority of *"Catholics"* in America believe it.

Several articles in the Constitution are completely at odds with the official teachings of the Catholic Church. This comes as no surprise.

The American Democracy was invented by the satanic organization of Freemasonry condemned by many popes. Many of the founding fathers were Freemasons, most probable, even the so-called Catholic family the Carrols. The first *"Americanist"* Bishop John Carrol, his brother Charles (friend of Benjamin Franklin,) and the notorious Daniel are all revered by American *"Catholics."*

To say the Republic was founded on Judeo-Christian values is ludicrous. First, Judaism is opposed to Christianity but not to Masonry. It was founded on Judeo-Masonic principles, not Christian.

This Freemasonic subversion of the Catholic State was warned by Pope Leo XIII in *Humanum genus*.

He declared in *Libertas Praestantissimum*, "To reject the supreme authority of God and to cast off all obedience to Him in public matters...is the greatest perversion of liberty."

Again, Pope St Pius X in his *letter to the Sillon*, "*a certain Democracy which goes so far in its wickedness as to place sovereignty in the people and aims at the suppression of classes and in their leveling down.*"

The heresy of Americanism has taken over the entire Church in America. We see signs of it everywhere. To name just a few examples:

American flags inside the churches sometimes right next to the altar, priests taking off from administering the sacraments on secular holidays such as Presidents Day and Martin Luther King Day, secular holidays coinciding and celebrated in Holy Mass or other Church functions such as Thanksgiving, Independence Day, and even Halloween, secular patriotic songs being sung at Holy Mass such as God bless America, the clergy supporting the nation's right to make moral laws democratically, placing the satanic image of the Statue of Liberty in the National Cathedral alongside of Our Lady who is the real Lady of Liberty, and supporting whole heartily a neo-Gnostic pro-choice/pro-Sodomite president.

Pope St Pius X spoke of, "*many who belong to the Catholic Laity, nay, and this is far more lamentable, to the ranks of the priesthood itself, who, FEIGNING A LOVE FOR THE CHURCH, lacking the firm protection of philosophy and theology, nay more, thoroughly imbued with the poisonous doctrines taught by the enemies of the Church and lost to all sense of modesty, vaunt themselves as reformers of the Church...They put their designs for her ruin into operation not from without but from within.*"

This brings us to the Second Vatican Council, when American bishops introduced the Americanist proposition that man has a right to be wrong.

I remember reading the passing of the Most Rev. Charles G. Maloney on April 30, 2006. He was the one responsible for my new rite Confirmation in 1983.

It was written of him after his funeral in the local diocesan newspaper *The Record*, that, *"He made a significant contribution at the Second Vatican Council to the development of the Declaration on Religious Freedom."*

Through the heresy of Americanism, came the introduction of the heresy of religious liberty. The document was finalized in 1965.

The document *Dignitatis Humanae* (Declaration of religious freedom) from Vatican 2 states:

*"This Vatican synod declares that the human person has a right to religious freedom. Such freedom consists in this, that all should have such immunity from coercion by individuals, or by groups, or by any human power, that no one should be force to act against his conscience in religious matters, nor prevented from acting according to his conscience, whether in private or in public, within due limits."*

*"Therefore this right to non-interference persists even in those who do not carry out their obligations of seeking the truth and standing by it; and the exercise of this right should not be curtailed, as long as due public order is preserved."*

This statement is declaring that man has a *"right"* to be wrong and contradicts the condemnation of proposition # 78 of *The Syllabus*.

In defense of this teaching, two strategies are used. The first is: *"There is no real contradiction. Vatican 2 is not saying that people should have the "right to error" but the right to worship God."*

The second is: *"Vatican 2 was not saying men have the moral right, but the civil right, especially now when there are no longer Catholic states."*

However, both arguments severely miss the point.

We all most certainly have a right to worship God, but Vatican 2 is saying everybody has a *"right"* to worship any god of one's choosing or falsely worship the true God in the public arena. Therefore, it is saying men have a 'right' to error, making it a contradiction to the official condemnation.

It does not matter if the government is non-Catholic or pagan. It would be inexcusable to say Satanism is a *"right."*

*The Syllabus of Errors* is infallible which means it cannot be altered in light of some condition such as false governments. Also, *The Syllabus* was not using situations or limits as a condition for it to apply only to Christian states.

Apologists will emphasize the documents wording that people cannot be coerced to follow or reject a particular religion because it is contrary to man's nature as being free.

However, the emphasis is not just that people cannot be coerced into a religion, but that erroneous actions cannot be prevented in public. Vatican 2 completely contradicts the historic Catholic teaching on this point. Again, *DH* 2 states: *"in religious matters, nor prevented from acting according to his conscience, whether in private or in public... the exercise of this right should not be curtailed..."*

Then we have *Dignitatis Humanae # 4:* *"In addition, religious communities are entitled to teach and give witness to their faith publicly in speech and writing without hindrance."*

This clearly contradicts Pope Gregory XVI, *Mirari Vos* (# 15), Aug. 15, 1832: *"Here We must include that harmful and never* sufficiently denounced freedom to publish any writings whatever and disseminate them to the people, which some dare to demand and promote with so great a clamor. We are horrified to see what monstrous doctrines and prodigious errors are disseminated far and wide in countless books, pamphlets, and other writings which, though small in weight, are very great in malice."

Pope Leo XIII, *Libertas* (# 42), June 20, 1888: *"From what has been said it follows that it is quite unlawful to demand, to defend, or to grant unconditional freedom of thought, of speech, or writing, or of worship, as if these were so many rights given by nature of man."*

Pope Leo XIII, *Immortale Dei* (# 34), Nov. 1, 1885: *"Thus, Gregory XVI in his encyclical letter Mirari Vos, dated August 15, 1832, inveighed with weighty words against the sophisms which even at his time were being publicly inculcated – namely, that no preference should be shown for any particular form of worship; that it is right for individuals to form their own personal judgments about religion; that each man's conscience is his sole and all-sufficing guide; and that it is lawful for every man to publish his own views, whatever they may be, and even to conspire against the state."*

Pope Pius IX, *Quanta Cura* (#'s 3-6), Dec. 8, 1864, *"From which totally false idea of social government they do not fear to foster that erroneous opinion, most fatal in its effects on the Catholic Church and the salvation of souls, called by Our predecessor, Gregory XVI, an insanity, namely, that 'liberty of conscience and worship is each man's personal right, which ought to be legally proclaimed and asserted in every rightly constituted society; and that a right resides in the citizens to an absolute liberty, which should be restrained by no authority whether ecclesiastical or civil, whereby they may be able openly and publicly to manifest and declare any of their ideas whatever, either by word of mouth, by the press, or in any other way. but while they rashly affirm this, they do not understand and note that they are preaching liberty of perdition... therefore, by our apostolic authority, we reprobate, proscribe, and condemn all the singular and evil opinions and doctrines specially mentioned in this letter, and will and command that they be thoroughly held by all the children of the catholic church as reprobated, proscribed and condemned."*

It is true that people should not be coerced but this is not the issue. Since the Catholic Church has solemnly declared that only the Catholic Church is keeping to true worship, then worshiping God in some other way, or worshiping false gods, and freely speaking and writing about it is not only error but serious error that will lead people to hell. Vatican 2 is advocating that man has a right to these errors.

John Paul I most clearly saw it when he stated, *"the Church had always taught that only the truth had rights, but now the Council made it clear that error also has rights." (Time Magazine)*

John Paul I voted at Vatican 2 knowing full well what Vatican 2 meant.

Finally, this heresy is blatantly contrary to the Papal Bull against Martin Luther.

*33. That heretics be burned is against the will of the Spirit.* CONDEMNED *as error of Martin Luther* in Bull *Exsurge Domine,* June 15, 1520 by Pope Leo X.

According to Vatican 2, it is contrary to the Spirit to burn heretics. Since man has a *right* to his own religion, the state could not burn him for simply being a heretic.

Vatican 2 agrees with the apostate Martin Luther and rejects Pope Leo X. How many today are in league with Luther on this point? However, practitioners of witchcraft were stoned in the Mosaic Law.

Ratzinger would later admit that Vatican 2 is contrary to the infallible teaching of Pope Pius IX.

> *"If one is looking for a global diagnosis of the text [of Gaudium et spes], one could say that it (along with the texts on religious liberty and world religions) is a revision of the Syllabus of Pius IX, a kind of counter-Syllabus ....*
>
> *Undoubtedly, many things have changed since then. The new ecclesiastical policy of Pius XI established a certain openness toward the liberal conception of the State. In a silent but persevering combat, Exegesis and Church History increasingly adopted the postulates of liberal science; on the other hand, in face of the great political upheavals of the 20th century, Liberalism was obliged to accept notable corrections.*
>
> *This happened because, first in central Europe, conditioned by the situation, the unilateral dependence on the positions taken by the Church through the initiatives of Pius IX and Pius X against the new period of History opened by the French Revolution was to a large extent corrected via facti. But a fundamental new document regarding relations with the world as it had been since 1789 was still lacking.*
>
> *In reality, the mentality that preceded the revolution still reigned in the countries with strong Catholic majorities; today almost no one denies that the Spanish and Italian concordats [accords between Church and State] tried to conserve too many things from a conception of the world that for a long time had not corresponded to reality. Likewise, almost no one can deny that this dependence on an obsolete conception of relations between the Church and State was matched by similar anachronisms in the domain of education and the attitude taken toward the modern historical-critical method ....*

*Let us content ourselves here with stating that the text [of Gaudium et spes] plays the role of a counter-Syllabus to the measure that it represents an attempt to officially reconcile the Church with the world as it had become after 1789. On one hand, this visualization alone clarifies the ghetto complex that we mentioned before. On the other hand, it permits us to understand the meaning of this new relationship between the Church and the Modern World. "World" is understood here, at depth, as the spirit of modern times. The consciousness of being a detached group that existed in the Church viewed this spirit as something separate from herself and, after the hot as well as cold wars were over, she sought dialogue and cooperation with it."* (From the French text: *Les Principes de la Theologie Catholique - Esquisse et Materiaux*, Paris: Tequi, 1982, pp. 426-427).

*"The task is not, therefore, to suppress the Council but to discover the real Council and to deepen its true intention in the light of present experience. That means that there can be no return to the Syllabus, which may have marked the first stage in the confrontation with liberalism and a newly conceived Marxism but cannot be the last stage."* (Ratzinger, *Principles of Catholic Theology*, 1982, p. 391)

Just as he confirmed in 1990 that the documents against modernism and religious liberty are obsolete, Ratzinger advocates that truth yesterday is not truth today. Rather than saying truth changes, he insinuates that it doesn't apply anymore. The world has gone beyond truth and now truth must be redefined to fit the changing world.

The mastermind behind the two documents *Dignitatis Humanae* and *Gaudium et spes*, mentioned by Ratizinger, was none other than his protégé, Bishop Wojtyła (John Paul II.)

Looking at *Gaudium et spes*, we see one of the pillars of civilization compromised; God and the relationship with man.

*Gaudium et Spes* – *Constitution on Church and the Modern World*

> *# 12: "According to the almost unanimous opinion of believers and unbelievers alike, all things on earth should be related to man as their center and crown."*
>
> *# 24: "This is why the first and greatest commandment is love of God and of neighbor."*
>
> *# 26: "There is also increasing awareness of the exceptional dignity which belongs to the human person, who is superior to everything and whose rights and duties are universal and inviolable."*

Notice how Vatican 2 builds up the dignity of man.

> "29 And Jesus answered him: The first commandment of all is, *Hear, O Israel: the Lord thy God is one God.*
> 30 *And thou shalt love the Lord thy God, with thy whole heart, and with thy whole soul, and with thy whole mind, and with thy whole strength.* This is the first commandment.
> 31 And the second is like to it: *Thou shalt love thy neighbour as thyself.* There is no other commandment greater than these." (Mark 12:29-31)

At face value, Vatican 2 is placing the dignity of man on the same plane as God.

Just how far are we to take the dignity of man? Above the justice of God?

Because of this new vision on the dignity of man, the death penalty is rejected by the new religion of Rome.

In the Old Covenant, the death penalty was charged by God as retribution against His Name and Authority. If a man murdered another, the capital punishment was pursued because the destruction of life was a crime against God first.

The Mosaic Law had many death penalties.

Taking the name of the Lord in vain was punishable by death because the holiness of God's name outweighs the dignity of human life.

The Ten Commandments are listed from the greatest to the least. The first three concern God and the next seven concern man. The greater the Commandment, the greater the crime and penalty attached.

Christ sums up the 10 Commandments into two. As all the Commandments relate to one another in one way or another, they are not equal.

God is first and man is second.

Historically, the Catholic Church has always recognized the right of the state to practice capital punishment. In fact, Pope St. Pius V promoted, encouraged, and even commanded that the death penalty be issued for certain crimes such as Sodomy.

However, the new religion doesn't recognize the superiority of God's dignity over man's dignity. They recognize both as being equal, and condemn the death penalty unless the individual becomes a threat within his society.

The second pillar of civilization; the Catholic Church itself is compromised by the Dogmatic Constitution *Lumen Gentium* of Vatican 2. It states:

*Chapter 1. The Mystery of the Church*

*This is the one Church of Christ which in the Creed is professed as one, holy, catholic and apostolic, (12\*) which our Saviour, after His Resurrection, commissioned Peter to shepherd, (74) and him and the other apostles to extend and direct with authority, (75) which He erected for all ages as "the pillar and mainstay of the truth". (76) This Church constituted and* *organized in the world as a society, subsists in the Catholic Church, which is governed by the successor of Peter and by the Bishops in communion with him, (13\*) although many elements of sanctification and of truth are found outside of its visible structure. These elements, as gifts belonging to the Church of Christ, are forces impelling toward catholic unity.*

Vatican 2 is redefining what the Church is.

To say that it subsists in the Catholic Church is to imply that it subsists elsewhere such as in non-Catholic churches.

When the Faithful say in the Nicene/Constantinopian Creed: I believe in One, Holy, Catholic, and Apostolic Church, we mean the whole Church of Christ, the Catholic Church, which is united, separated from the world, universal, and from the Apostles. The Councils of Nicea and Constantinople expounded the Apostle's Creed I believe *"the Holy Catholic Church."* These are articles of Faith and must be believed as the Church has always taught.

The four marks: One, Holy, Catholic, and Apostolic describe the Catholic Church.

However, Vatican 2 is saying the four marks are describing the Church of Christ, which, according to *LG*, only subsists in the Catholic Church. This is precisely the same belief of those Protestants who recite the same creed.

Vatican 2 expounds on the principle that the Church of Christ only subsists in the Catholic Church:

*The people of God (LG Ch 2.)*

*15. "For several reasons the Church recognizes that it is joined to those who, though baptized and so honored with the Christian name, do not profess the faith in its entirety or do not preserve communion under the successor of St. Peter."*

The new religion recognizes heretics and schismatics as people of God.

Pope Pius IX, *Amantissimus* (# 3), April 8, 1862: *"There are other, almost countless, proofs drawn from the most trustworthy witnesses which clearly and openly testify with great faith, exactitude, respect and obedience that all who want to belong to the true and only Church of Christ must honor and obey this Apostolic See and the Roman Pontiff."*

Pope Pius VI, *Charitas* (# 32), April 13, 1791: *"Finally, in one word, stay close to Us. For no one can be in the Church of Christ without being in unity with its visible head and founded on the See of Peter."*

Notice that the Church of Christ is the Catholic Church.

Pope Leo XIII, *Satis Cognitum* (# 13), June 29, 1896: *"Therefore if a man does not want to be, or to be called, a heretic, let him not strive to please this or that man... but let him hasten before all things to be in communion with the Roman See."*

Notice again, not to be in communion with the Roman See is to be called heretic.

According to Vatican 2, the true Church of Christ is not united as one religion nor is it catholic or universal. This is a rejection of two Articles of Faith.

*"It follows that these separated churches and communities as such, though we believe them to be deficient in some respects, have by no means been deprived of significance and importance in the mystery of salvation. For the Spirit of Christ has not refrained from using them as means of salvation whose efficacy comes from that fullness of grace and truth which has been entrusted to the Catholic Church."* (Vatican 2, *UR 3*)

This means these other churches are good enough for salvation however contrary to several papal teachings.

Pope Leo XIII, *Satis Cognitum* (# 9), June 29, 1896: *"The Church alone offers to the human race that religion – that state of absolute perfection – which He wished, as it were, to be incorporated in it. And it alone supplies those means of salvation which accord with the ordinary counsels of Providence."*

Pope Pius X, *Editae saepe* (# 29), May 26, 1910: *"The Church alone possesses together with her magisterium the power of governing and sanctifying human society. Through her ministers and servants (each in his own station and office), she confers on mankind suitable and necessary means of salvation."*

Pope Eugene IV, Council of Florence, *"Cantate Domino,"* 1441, ex cathedra: *"The Holy Roman Church firmly believes, professes and preaches that all those who are outside the Catholic Church, not only pagans but also Jews or heretics and schismatics, cannot share in eternal life and will go into the everlasting fire which was prepared for the Devil and his angels, unless they are joined to the Church before the end of their lives ..."*

Pope Clement VI, *Super quibusdam,* Sept. 20, 1351: *"We ask: In the first place, whether you and the Church of the Armenians which is obedient to you, believe that all those who in baptism have received the same Catholic faith, and afterwards have withdrawn and will withdraw in the future from the communion of this same Roman Church, which one alone is Catholic, are schismatic and heretical, if they remain obstinately separated from the faith of this Roman Church."*

Pope Leo XIII, *Satis Cognitum* (# 9), June 29, 1896: *"The practice of the Church has always been the same, as is shown by the unanimous teaching of the Fathers, who were wont to hold as outside Catholic communion, and alien to the Church, whoever would recede in the least degree from any point of doctrine proposed by her authoritative magisterium."*

According to Vatican 2, since these non-Catholic heretical and schismatic churches are part of the Church of Christ, *"are a means of salvation", "live the life of grace", "build up", "give life"* and *"help grow"* the true Church, then it must follow that we treat each other equally.

Equality was one on the foundations of the French Revolution.

The document *Unitatis Redintegratio* of Vatican 2 states:

*Chapter 2. The practice of ecumenism*

*9. "We must get to know the outlook of our separated fellow Christians... Most valuable for this purpose are meetings of the two sides – especially for discussion of theological problems – where each side can treat with the other on an equal footing, provided that those who take part in them under the guidance of their authorities are truly competent."*

This contradicts Pope Pius XI in *Mortalium Animos* (# 7), Jan. 6, 1928, speaking of heretics: *"Meanwhile they affirm that they would willingly treat with the Church of Rome, but on equal terms, that is as equals with an equal."*

Later, paragraphs 13-15 of *UR*, Ch 3, titled *"Churches and ecclesial communities separated from the Roman apostolic see"* of Vatican 2 clearly teaches that schismatic churches are part of the Church of Christ.

It is argued that the Congregation for the Doctrine of the Faith (CDF) teaches that *"subsists"* means *"alone and retains all"* or *"belongs uniquely and exclusively"* and *"to absolutely no other"* and *"alone."* Therefore, Vatican 2 is not teaching a heretical doctrine.

Subsist is defined as: (a.) To exist; be. (b.) To remain or continue in existence. To attribute this word to mean or indicate as *"belongs uniquely and exclusively"* and *"to absolutely no other"* and *"alone"* is so ridiculous

Vatican 2 gives a word so false, so erroneous, that it takes us to have to ask what does this mean, because the face value of this word doesn't square up.

The word *"subsists"* does not mean what the CDF says it means. The definition of this word is clear and this definition, (not some definition that the CDF creates out of the word) is heretical. It is a simple definition and it is completely ridiculous for the CDF to try to cover up the plain meaning of the word.

Again, the word *"subsists"* is defined other than what the CDF suggests and John Paul II and Benedict have also spoken differently about it. Vatican 2 is heretical by its words. Interpretation is something else. There is no universal and ordinary magisterial interpretation of *"subsists."*

If the CDF is correct, then you still have Vatican 2 itself saying that other false churches are a means of salvation when *"outside the Church there is no salvation"* therefore false churches must be part of the Church of Christ. This means that Vatican 2 is at best contradicting itself.

Lastly, one must admit the word is obscure. It's ambiguous at best. This means Vatican 2 at best created a serious doubt, which the Catholic Church cannot do. The fact that the CDF had to clarify it proves that *"subsists"* is the wrong word, thus it makes for a heretical phrase.

Perhaps, the greatest aspect of the apostasy of Rome is the fact that they recognize as people who worship the one true God those who reject Christ as God. This is taught in the Dogmatic Constitution *Lumen Gentium* Ch. 2 titled "*The people of God.*" It states:

*16. "But the plan of salvation also embraces those who acknowledge the Creator, and among these the Muslims are first; they profess to hold the faith of Abraham and along with us they worship the one merciful God who will judge mankind on the last day."*

This statement is saying by implication that the rejection of Christ is not a rejection of the one true God.

Pope St. Damasus I, Council of Rome, Can. 15: *"If anyone does not say that he (Jesus Christ)...will come to judge the living and the dead, he is a heretic."*

Vatican 2 confirms *LG* in *Nostra aetate* (Declaration on the church's relation to non-Christian religions):

*3. "The Church also looks upon Muslims with respect. They worship the one God living and subsistent, merciful and mighty, creator of heaven and earth, who has spoken to humanity and to whose decrees, even the hidden ones, they seek to submit themselves whole-heartedly, just as Abraham, to whom the Islamic faith readily relates itself, submitted to God...Hence they have regard for the moral life and worship God in prayer, almsgiving and fasting."*

The problem with this declaration is that it doesn't matter what the claim Muslims hold to profess, but what they actually profess. They reject Christ and the Trinity and therefore do not *"actually"* hold to the faith of Abraham. They reject the one true God.

St. John in chapter 8 writes about Jesus condemning those who claim to hold the faith of Abraham. Jesus says their father is the Devil because they do not believe the truth of the Gospel. The Muslims reject the Gospels meaning they are in the same boat as the Jews whom Christ condemns.

As a matter of fact, this statement of Vatican 2 is the doctrine of antichrist. St. John says anyone who denies that Jesus is the Christ is the antichrist and there are many of them. Muslims deny Jesus as God and Messiah, which means they are all antichrists with the backing of Vatican II.

The fact is Muslims worship a false god they call Allah or God. He is not the Holy Trinity but a devil. The religion was founded by Mohammed who claimed that the angel Gabriel gave him the Koran as the holy book for the newfound religion.

However, we have been warned of such a thing.

*"But though we, or an angel from heaven, preach a gospel to you besides that which we have preached to you, let him be anathema."*(Gal. 1:8)

The *"we"* and *"angel"* refer to those who come as Apostles or holy Angels in name only but in reality are cons and Devils.

It is argued that Muslims worship the one true God but have a false understanding of Him. The same is said of most all monotheistic religions. Does this mean that Ahura Mazda of Zoroastrianism is really the one true God but just a false understanding of Him?

Why could this argument not work for any religion that has one high god with perhaps lesser gods?

Interestingly enough, these pagan religions are encouraged by the new religion of Rome. The Assisi Events in 1986 and 2002 were invitations by Rome and specifically John Paul II to the religious leaders of their respective pagan sects to pray to their pagan gods for world peace. In 2006, Benedict celebrated the 20th anniversary of the Events and hailed it as a great achievement.

John Paul II has participated numerous times in non-Catholic worship services. Once in 1986 in India, while wearing Zoroastrian garb, he actually practiced the pagan religion.

Psalm 95 has now been reversed in the new religion, for it is no longer, *"For all the gods of the Gentiles are Devils,"* but rather all gods are God.

The new religion of Rome rejects, *"But the things which the heathens sacrifice, they sacrifice to Devils, and not to God. And I would not that you should be partakers with Devils."*(I Cor. 10:20)

Rather, they now encourage, promote and take part in the worship of non-Catholic ceremonies. If the new religion of Rome believed (Psalm 95 and I Cor. 10:20) applied to today's pagans, would they have invited them to Assisi to worship Devils? Perhaps they would only for the world to hold that they are not Devils but God.

Numerous Articles of Faith have been rejected or redefined by the new religion of man.

These Articles of Faith found in the Apostles' Creed which Vatican 2 redefined is a condemned error of modernists.

Pope St. Pius X: *62. The principal articles of the Apostles' Creed did not have the same meaning for the Christians of the earliest times as they have for the Christians of our time. CONDEMNED as an error of the Modernists,* by Pope St. Pius X in *Lamentabili,* July 3, 1907.

Vatican 2 new understanding of the sacred dogmas of the Creed also falls under the condemnation of Vatican 1, which stated:

Vatican 1, Session 3, April 24, 1870 Chapter 4 *"On Faith and Reason" For the doctrine of the faith which God has revealed is put forward not as some philosophical discovery capable of being perfected by human intelligence, but as a divine deposit committed to the spouse of Christ to be faithfully protected and infallibly promulgated. Hence, too, that meaning of the sacred dogmas is ever to be maintained which has once been declared by holy mother church, and there must never be any abandonment of this sense under the pretext or in the name of a more profound understanding. May understanding, knowledge and wisdom increase as ages and centuries roll along, and greatly and vigorously flourish, in each and all, in the individual and the whole church: but this only in its own proper kind, that is to say, in the same doctrine, the same sense, and the same understanding."*

Paul VI once said in his general audience on July 2, 1969, *"If the world changes, should not religion also change? It is for this very reason that the Church has, especially after the Second Vatican Council, undertaken so many forms."*

Yet, Pope St. Pius X in *Lamentabili*, July 3, 1907 Condemned the following as an error of the Modernists: *53. The organic constitution of the Church is not immutable; but Christian society, just as human society, is subject to perpetual evolution.*

The purpose of Vatican 2 was to change the organic constitution of the Church to fit modern society.

None of the Vatican 2 popes took the oath against modernism since Paul VI had abolished it. But why abolish it? As Ratzinger said, it doesn't apply anymore.

So that you have a clear understanding what Ratzinger and the rest of the Vatican 2 *"papal"* gang believes, the following oath will be presented in order that you see what it is they reject.

## The Oath Against the Errors of Modernism by Pope St. Pius X, Sept. 1, 1910:

*"I....firmly embrace and accept all and everything that has been defined, affirmed, and declared by the unerring magisterium of the Church. ...I reject the heretical invention of the evolution of dogmas, passing from one meaning to another... I disapprove the error of those who affirm that the faith proposed by the Church can be in conflict with history, and that Catholic dogmas, in the sense in which they are now understood, cannot be reconciled with the more authentic origins of the Catholic religion"*

The new 1992 Catechism of the Catholic Church does not reference any of St. Pius X writings that solemnly condemn modernism. The greatest pope in the last 500 years and his greatest achievement are completely rejected by the new modernist religion of Rome. Rather, the new religion believes it just doesn't apply anymore.

Since it doesn't apply anymore, then Vatican 2 took the next step by revising most of the traditional religious observances including all seven of the sacraments.

*Sacrosanctum Concilium #63b:* *"There is to be a new edition of the Roman book of rites, and, following this as a model, each competent local church authority (see article 22.2) should prepare its own, adapted to the needs of individual areas, including those to do with language, as soon as possible."*

*#66:* *"Both rites of adult baptism are to be revised, the simpler one and the more elaborate one, the latter with reference to the renewed catechumenate."*

*#67:* *"The rite of infant baptism is to be revised, and adapted to the reality of the situation with babies."*

*#71:* *"The rite of confirmation is also to be revised."*

*#72:* *"The rites and formulas of penance are also to be revised in such a way that they express more clearly what the sacrament is and what it brings about."*

*#76:* *"The rites for different kinds of ordination are to be revised – both the ceremonies and the texts."*

*#77:* *"The rite of celebrating marriage in the Roman book of rites is to be revised, and made richer, in such a way that it will express the grace of the sacrament more clearly...."*

*#79:* *"The sacramentals should be revised... the revision should also pay attention to the needs of our time."*

*#80:* *"The rite of consecration of virgins found in the Roman pontifical is to be subjected to review."*

*#82:* "The rite of burying little children should be revised, and a special mass provided."

*#89d:* "The hour of prime is to be suppressed."

*#93:* "... the hymns are to be restored to their original form. Things which smack of mythology or which are less suited to Christian holiness are to be removed or changed."

*#107:* "The liturgical year is to be revised."

*#128:* "The ecclesiastical canons and statutes which deal with the provision of visible things for worship are to be revised as soon as possible."

Head coverings for women, one of the prime practices of Catholicism based on a fundamental doctrine is no longer found in the new religion for the small exception of those attempting to recognize the new religion alongside the historic.

Almighty God through St. Paul clearly and unambiguously taught that head coverings are to be practiced in the Catholic Church.

*"1 Be ye followers of me, as I also am of Christ.*
*2 Now I praise you, brethren, that in all things you are mindful of me: and keep my ordinances as I have delivered them to you.*
*3 But I would have you know, that the head of every man is Christ; and the head of the woman is the man; and the head of Christ is God.*
*4 Every man praying or prophesying with his head covered, disgraceth his head.*
*5 But every woman praying or prophesying with her head not covered, disgraceth her head: for it is all one as if she were shaven.*
*6 For if a woman be not covered, let her be shorn. But if it be a shame to a woman to be shorn or made bald, let her cover her head.*

103

*7 The man indeed ought not to cover his head, because he is the image and glory of God; but the woman is the glory of the man.*

*8 For the man is not of the woman, but the woman of the man.*

*9 For the man was not created for the woman, but the woman for the man.*

*10 Therefore ought the woman to have a power over her head, because of the angels.*

*11 But yet neither is the man without the woman, nor the woman without the man, in the Lord.*

*12 For as the woman is of the man, so also is the man by the woman; but all things of God."* (I Cor 11:1-12)

According to the natural law argument that Holy Scripture uses, head coverings are to be worn as a sign that a woman is under the authority of a man (1 Cor 11:1-16; 1 Cor 14:33-38; 1 Tim 2:11-15; Col. 3:18; Eph. 5:22-33; Tit. 2:5; 1 Peter 3:1-5).

Since the natural law was used as an *apologia*, then by logical extension, head coverings for women is a divine mandate from God from the very beginning. It is actually built into creation. It is not a mere cultural practice.

St. Paul emphatically stated, *"So brethren, stand firm and hold fast to the traditions which you have been taught by us..."* (II Thess. 2:15)

We have just seen St Paul tell the Corinthians that head coverings is a Tradition.

Now this Tradition is disregarded as a cultural practice for ancient times which is not appropriate in our day and age.

Christ said that His Word will never pass away even though the world would. Head coverings are not just St. Paul's word but Christ's Word which will never pass away.

These uncovered women now speak in the churches of the holy one as lector *esses* 'also forbidden by St. Paul in Holy Writ. (I Cor. 14:33-36, I Tim. 2:8-15)

Since the implantation of the Second Vatican Council, the whole Catholic world disappeared in a blink of an eye.

Everything changed with new doctrines (heresies), new practices (previously condemned evil disciplines), new worship services, with a different mentality of the Church, government, and the world.

A Catholic from the 19th Century would never recognize the new religion of the late 20th Century. Yet, he would have no problem recognizing it every century prior. The reason, of course, is because the new religion is just that. A NEW RELIGION!

This is the apostasy of today.

The world invited in modernism and it won and now *"Catholics"* including Protestants (earlier modernists) think they are pleasing God as they believe, do, and think as modernists.

Christ told his true followers how to indentify false teachers and prophets, *"Beware of false prophets, who come to you in the clothing of sheep, but inwardly they are ravening wolves.
By their fruits you shall know them."* (Matt. 7:15-16)

What are the fruits of John XXIII through Benedict XVI and their Vatican Council?

The priesthood was at an all time high before the Council in America with approximately 60,000. Now, it is below 45,000. Ordinations also declined 350%. As the population has greatly increased over the last 40 years, the Church greatly decreased immediately following the Council with far fewer seminarians, nuns, religious, Catholic schools and students, and converts. Mass attendance dropped somewhere between 25% and 50%.

The things that did increase were annulments, priests leaving the priesthood, and Catholics converting over to the Mormons, Watchtower Society, and Protestantism, Evangelicalism, and Fundamentalism.

For all the major changes that came about with the new religion, there came about a great increase of liturgical abuses even from the perspective and standard of the new religion.

While all these things have taken place with no end in sight, the false prophets of the new religion of Rome are trying to convince their blind followers that we are in the *"new springtime"* for the church.

This is a half-truth.

It is certainly a new springtime for the new ape church, but not for the Catholic Church which has been reduced to a remnant.

And so the lie keeps the followers of the new religion safely within her bosom.

Again, Exorcist Fr. Malachi Martin reported that Satan was enthroned as head of the Church inside the Vatican during the middle of the Second Vatican Council and the night before Paul VI's coronation and believed the Vatican is now possessed!

He was right!

The religion of God in Rome was usurped and has been replaced by the new religion of man spreading throughout the world and doing so in the name of God.

Identification of different religions is based on what they believe, teach, and practice.

Under the guise of modernism, the Vatican 2 Church is no doubt Satan's grand masterpiece.

The Devil could not have better orchestrated his ape church as he usurped the Catholic Church mocking her every sacrament. For every heresy and blasphemy that is spewed out of the Vatican 2 documents and her popes, their defenders actually justify in the name of our Lord as great teachings given by the Holy Ghost. This is an astounding feat even for the Devil. However, we know that all of Satan's power was given him by God for God's greater glory.

In the end, the Catholic Church will triumph over Her enemies at the Second Coming.

# The Antichrist

Much has been written about the antichrist with numerous speculations as to who he will be.

The term antichrist is only used four times in Holy Scripture:

> "Little children, it is the last hour; and as you have heard that Antichrist cometh, even now there are become many Antichrists: whereby we know that it is the last hour." (I John 2:18)

> "Who is a liar, but he who denieth that Jesus is the Christ? This is Antichrist, who denieth the Father, and the Son" (I John 2:22)

> "And every spirit that dissolveth Jesus, is not of God: and this is Antichrist, of whom you have heard that he cometh, and he is now already in the world."(I John 4:3)

> "For many seducers are gone out into the world, who confess not that Jesus Christ is come in the flesh: this is a seducer and an antichrist." (II John 1:7)

St. John specifically identifies that an antichrist is coming and yet he says they have now come making the last hour.

St. Paul also gives us several hints about the antichrist in (II Thess. 2:3-11).

The antichrist will be revealed immediately after the apostasy.

He opposes and is lifted up above God, or worshipped as he sits in the temple as if he were God.

The mystery of iniquity is the spirit of antichrist and is already working.

He will be revealed after someone is gone or removed.

He will be a deception, his works will be a deception, and those who reject the truth will believe the deception.

The question is how one will know that the final antichrist is indeed the final antichrist?

How the antichrist sits as if he were God can't be obvious otherwise no one would listen or follow him. He must be very conspicuous, and indeed the world will not recognize him.

The Faithful must always be ready because antichrist is here. This is why Holy Scripture has it for men to always be on guard.

The final antichrist will simply be unrecognizable.

When St. Peter refers to the Second Coming, he almost immediately states, *"Be sober, and watch: because your adversary, the Devil, as a roaring lion, goeth about, seeking whom he may devour."* (I Peter 5:4, 8)

Christ warns several times to be ready and watch for you know not the hour. (Matt. 24:44, 25:13, Luke 12:40)

What is most striking is that Christ does not mention a final antichrist to come before the consummation of the world.

This is a valuable insight.

If the knowledge of antichrist is of such importance wouldn't Jesus mention this detail? The Catechism of Trent borrowed from Christ's words about the preaching of the Gospel throughout the world as one of the final signs before the end, and did so from chapter 24 of the Gospel of Matthew no less.

Perhaps Christ doesn't mention antichrist for the simple fact that he would not be recognized when he indeed comes. What Jesus does tell us is, *"many false prophets shall rise, and shall seduce many."*(Matt. 24:11)

*"For there shall arise false christs and false prophets, and shall show great signs and wonders, insomuch as to deceive (if possible) even the elect.*
*Behold I have told it to you, beforehand."*(Matt. 24:24-25)

Jesus is implying that even the elect most probably will not recognize antichrist when he comes. They will not be deceived into following the antichrist but will be deceived as to who he will be.

St. John then gives us his Apocalypse which speaks about the antichrist through implication under the identification of the scarlet beast.

St. John never says that the beast is a single man but rather implies that it is more than just one man.

The belief in one final antichrist has a better foundation in St. Paul's Epistle.

Because St. Paul's references in his Epistle the phrase *"son of perdition,"* it must be reckoned that his statement is also apocalyptic. He deliberately chose the phrase knowing full well from which is came. This expression is symbolic.

In Verse 3, St. Paul says that *"the man of sin be revealed"* is also *"the son of perdition."*

In Verse 8, St. Paul says that the *"wicked one shall be revealed"* is the same as *"the man of sin"* and *"the son of perdition."*

The son of perdition is Judas (John 17:12), but here St. Paul is referring to the spirit of Judas which is betrayal for that wicked one.

Christ shed his blood for the whole world, but man would betray Christ for what He did for them.

The wicked one and son of perdition is revealed by way of Verses 9-10, *"Whose coming is according to the working of Satan, in all power, and signs, and lying wonders,*
*And in all seduction of iniquity to them that perish: Because they receive not the love of the truth that they might be saved. Therefore God shall send them the operation of error, to believe a lie."*

Powers, signs, and lying wonders are explained in the next chapter that will deal with the Apocalypse of St. John.

His vision is a recapitulation of the same crucial events that affect civilization. Time is not always in order.

For instance, (Apocalypse 12:6) speaks about the woman who fled into the wilderness which was told to be Israel of the New Covenant or the Church. The next two verses speak about St. Michael defeating the Dragon and his angels casting them out of heaven. The events of verse 6 happened long after the events of verses 7 and 8, at least as we are concerned. Eternal time and our time are different.

This must be kept in mind when reading the last book of the most Holy Bible.

Since it has been historically understood that St. John wrote the book under the reign of Domitian sometime around 96 AD, the prophetic events take place in the future.

# The Beasts of the Apocalypse

This study already identified the two witnesses in the Apocalypse which leads us to the beasts.

*"And when they shall have finished their testimony, the beast, that ascendeth out of the abyss, shall make war against them, and shall overcome them, and kill them."* (Apocalypse 11:7)

Notice that Satan rules from the bottom up.

As previously noted, the two witnesses do not have to be understood as literally two individuals, but rather symbols of Christian martyrs down through the ages under the spirits of Elias, Enoch, Moses, etc.

Therefore, the beast properly understood in this verse is the spirit of the antichrist that St. John and St. Paul refers to that is already working in the world.

The following commentary of the Apocalypse will help develop maybe how the beast ought to be understood.

The Apocalypse in chapter 13 reads:

*1 And I saw a beast coming up out of the sea, having seven heads and ten horns, and upon his horns ten diadems, and upon his heads names of blasphemy.*

Like the Dragon in chapter 12, this beast has seven heads and ten horns, but the horns have ten diadems, when the Dragon has seven diadems on the heads.

The diadems represent sovereignty and power. In chapter 12, the Dragon is a *"sign"* as the woman is a *"sign."* The woman represents the Church and the Dragon represents Satan, the Devil who has been given dominion over the earth. The beast is the visible force of the Devil who is the invisible head of the beast.

The heads represent ages of time and horns represent kings, which in turn represent the nations of the world.

The number seven represents perfection and unity and ten is a whole number representing completion.

(Apocalypse 17:15) states, *"The waters that you saw...are peoples and multitudes and nations and tongues."* The beast comes out of these *"waters"* that make up the sea.

Therefore, the beast represents the spirit of antichrist found in the conglomeration of men of this world of nations, governments, and false religions.

*2 And the beast, which I saw, was like to a leopard, and his feet were as the feet of a bear, and his mouth as the mouth of a lion. And the dragon gave him his own strength, and great power.*

As the beasts in Daniel, this beast has many different qualities representing different powers. The beast operates in four different modes of life: Religion, politics, economics, and education.

*3 And I saw one of his heads as it were slain to death: and his death's wound was healed. And all the earth was in admiration after the beast.*

Israel that rejected its Messiah is the head which received the death wound. It happened at the destruction of the temple in 70 AD. Since St. John is writing his Apocalypse in the 90's, he is looking back in time at the event.

It appeared that Israel was destroyed but wasn't. It continued on persecuting the Church. It even had its own council at Javneh (Jamnia) in 90 AD which cast out the Holy Scriptures of the deuterocanonical books of the Septuagint Bible used by Christ.

The true Jewish religion is Christianity. The counterfeit Jewish religion (Judaism of today) is the *"synagogue of Satan."* (Apocalypse 2:9, 3:9)

The counterfeit religion carries with it the spirit of antichrist which is the epitome of the beast. Therefore, this beast against Christ is what the earth was in admiration of.

*4 And they adored the dragon, which gave power to the beast: and they adored the beast, saying: Who is like to the beast? and who shall be able to fight with him?*

The dragon or Satan was in control of all kingdoms of the world and their glory. This is why as the third temptation, Satan offered to give Christ those kingdoms if only He bowed down and worshipped him.

Satan was then crushed by the *"woman."* (Gen. 3:15) Our Lady's fiat brought Christ into the world. Christ's death and resurrection resulted in an angel chaining Satan in the bottomless pit or hell until he will be released for one final battle. (Apocalypse 20:3-4)

This Angel is the restraining one St. Paul was referring in (II Thess. 2:6). When the dragon or Satan is released, he will possess his visible counterpart which is the beast who will then perform great signs and wonders to deceive if possible even the elect. (Matt. 24:24, Apocalypse 13:13-15) Antichrist is the seed of the serpent. (Gen. 3:15)

Diabolical possession in individuals throughout history is a foreshadowing of the great possession over the men of the world at the end of time.

Although Satan is not three persons nor does he have the power to make himself a man as God, none-the-less he tries to mock God with his own type of anti-trinity. Satan, antichrist, and spirit of antichrist make up this anti-Trinity.

Just as Christ sent the Holy Spirit upon the Church giving its members the supernatural gifts of wisdom, understanding, counsel, fortitude, knowledge, piety, and fear of the Lord, so too, Satan sends his spirit of antichrist upon the world giving it natural gifts.

The Holy Spirit is revealed through Christians by their good fruits such as charity, joy, peace, patience, goodness, modesty, etc.

The spirit of antichrist is revealed through the bad of fruits of mankind.

Just as Christians spread the Gospel to bring men out of the world into Christ, so too, antichrist will attempt to keep men aloof and ignorant.

Since man with the spirit of antichrist will be arrogant and prideful, he will produce those great signs and wonders to deceive himself and Christians. However, those Christians predestined to salvation known as the elect will not be lost.

The deception is the worship of self.

Great signs and wonders today began with electricity and the industrial revolution and later advancing to include genetic engineering, cloning, super advance avionics, rockets and space stations, the harnessing of nuclear power, nanotechnology, super advance computer and special effects technology, weapons of mass destruction, test tube babies to the Hadron Collider , and who knows what else?

Christ once made a great storm cease at the sound of His Voice. Now, man can create the storm.

Man has solved and is solving the problems of the world leading him to think so highly of himself that he will ultimately place his dignity on an equal basis with God giving Him no credit and no glory for the human achievements.

This adoration of self may not be apparent in the sense of adoration giving in churches and temples. Rather, a general adoration of all that hell represents and presents in the men of the world.

Antichrist is gradually revealed making him conspicuous.

*5 And there was given to him a mouth speaking great things, and blasphemies; and power was given to him to do two and forty months.*

Elias stopped the rain for one-thousand two-hundred and sixty days which is forty-two months.

Christ preached for three and half years which is forty-two months. The number symbolizes the time of preaching of Christ, which the Church (the Body of Christ) does in fulfilling Her mission.

Daniel designated the time of the abomination of desolation to take place after the sacrifice is taken away as a thousand two-hundred and ninety days which is forty-three months and a month longer than the other times given. (Dan.12:11) Then states in verse 12: *"Blessed is he that waiteth and cometh unto a thousand three hundred thirty-five days."*

Numbers should never be taken literally in the apocalyptic writings. They almost always have symbolic meanings.

In the Apocalypse, the phrase *"one-thousand two-hundred and sixty days"* is used twice. That time frame given for the beast to operate is the same amount of time as the two witnesses spreading the Gospel (11:3) and the woman being nourished during her flight in the wilderness (12:6). In other words, the beast or the visible operation of Satan works to destroy the woman (Church) throughout her life with her members (two witnesses) giving their lives in testimony to the Gospel.

117

After 1260 days, the Church apostatizes and her mission comes to a screeching halt being reduced to a remnant.

Daniel's time is referencing that time after the 1260 days. An abomination will take place after the beast's operation. The time 1260 days to the 1290 days is the time of antichrist which is the beast now possessed by Satan who was just let loose from the bottomless pit. The 1335 days is referencing the time of the Second Coming and destruction of antichrist.

While the beast is operating, Satan is chained until he is released for his final assault. He will then be manifested as he possesses the men of the world thus revealing antichrist. His time will be short (Apocalypse 12:12, 20:3) and then Christ finally conquers all. The 1260 to 1335 is that short period of Satan's final assault.

For this reason Christ tells his followers to endure until the end that they may be saved. (Matt. 24:13)

The next several verses reinforce the final assault and again stating, *"Here is a call for the endurance and faith of the saints."*

Then we come to verse eleven...

*11 And I saw another beast coming up out of the earth, and he had two horns, like a lamb, and he spoke as a dragon.*

The first beast comes out of the sea of man, and the second comes out of the land of ideas and philosophies since land also comes out of the sea. Both sea and land represents the whole world.

Two beasts are given as mockers of the two witnesses: two witnesses for East and West and two beasts from sea and land. Both represent the whole earth.

Two Horns represents kingship as they did for Daniel in chapter 8:20. However, the lamb represents Christ and in this case a false christ or false religion. Authority and religion are ultimately what the marks represent. Since he speaks as a dragon with a type of authority mocking Christ, this beast represents false religions in general. False religions are authoritative and are in union against Christianity.

The second beast is also called the false prophet in chapters 16:13, 19:20 and 20:10.

*12 And he executed all the power of the former beast in his sight; and he caused the earth, and them that dwell therein, to adore the first beast, whose wound to death was healed.*

This false prophet which represents that which pertains to religion has the same type of authority as the first beast. The spirit of antichrist and man make up the beast. Men of the world create the false religions. These religions in turn have men worshipping themselves as is evident of the fact that man invents the doctrines of their respected religions. By doing so, they reject the doctrines of Christ and therefore, make themselves false christs and false prophets with an authority like Christ.

The first beast that represents the antichrist sits in the temple of God according to St. Paul.

Spiritually speaking, the temple could represent the hearts of man since man is the temple of God. St. John speaks about those who take on the character of the antichrist in chapter 16, verse 2. This character of antichrist explains how the antichrist could sit in the temple as if he were God since men of the world believe or hold themselves up as God in his heart.

Chapter 16:10 mentions the seat of the beast which is in the temple of God.

Pope St. Pius X implies that the universe is the temple of God and it is man who places himself *"in the place of God, raising himself above all that is called God; in such wise that although he cannot utterly extinguish in himself all knowledge of God, he has contemned God's majesty and, as it were, made of the universe a temple wherein he himself is to be adored."*

Man is the antichrist!

Christ spoke to his followers, *"If you had been of the world, the world would love its own; but because you are not of the world, but I have chosen you out of the world, therefore the world hateth you."* (John 15:19)

The men of this world form the antichrist.

Christ was clear when he spoke, *"He that is not with me, is against me; and he that gathereth not with me, scattereth."* (Luke 11:23)

All men not in Christ through rejection of Him is the antichrist.

Just as the Church is the Mystical Body of Christ, so too, Satan has a mystical body which is the spirit of antichrist in man.

The Church of Christ is referred to as a *"woman"* because she is the Bride of Christ. She is the woman of faith!

Because Satan has no real bride, the mystical body of Satan is a perversion of the sacrament of marriage, therefore his body is what makes up the *"man of sin."*

This mystical body of the Devil and Satan is made up of men of all false religions, secret societies, dictatorships, false governments, and schools of thought that contradict the dogmas and doctrines of Christianity.

The temple is the universe.

A literal interpretation of the temple could only mean the Catholic Church since anything else would not be a temple of God. If the temple of Jerusalem is rebuilt, it could not be considered the temple of God as it would not be for God but rather for the Devil, the flesh and the world.

This seat in the temple of God would be the papacy.

Protestants, such as its founder Luther, who considered the pope as the antichrist never realized that by holding to such a position, would necessarily imply that the papacy is the seat in the temple of God of which they rejected. Therefore, Protestants condemned themselves with this position.

A false pope pretending to be pope would be the most excellent way if possible to deceive the elect. (Matt. 24:24, Mark 13:22)

This interpretation is not only found within Protestantism, but also in historic Catholicism. See Appendix 1 – Catholic Prophecies about the Apostasy.

Is this literal interpretation the one that St. John had envisioned?

I would think not, although there is no reason to reject a type of literal interpretation given since the mystery of salvation history could include such a thing. Just as the destruction of the temple in 70 AD represents a type of literal events that will take place at the consummation of the world, so too, the figurative language of the Apocalypse could come about in a literal sense. Therefore, secondary interpretations are possible. Some of the Catholic prophecies also confirm the symbolic interpretation.

The next several verses are apocalyptic language used to symbolize power and deception.

> *13 And he did great signs, so that he made also fire to come down from heaven unto the earth in the sight of men.*

This is a mockery of the two witnesses who also do great signs. Elias also called down fire from Heaven on Mt. Carmel. Moses turned water into blood, and St. Peter walked by the sick that his shadow healed them. (Acts 5:15) Many more examples could be given.

> *14 And he seduced them that dwell on the earth, for the signs, which were given him to do in the sight of the beast, saying to them that dwell on the earth, that they should make the image of the beast, which had the wound by the sword, and lived.*

This would not necessarily mean an outright idolatry image but one reflecting all that the beast is about. Technology, science, media venues, medicine, schools and universities that work against the glory of God is an image of the beast.

> *15 And it was given him to give life to the image of the beast, and that the image of the beast should speak; and should cause, that whosoever will not adore the image of the beast, should be slain.*

This image that speaks symbolizes how technology, media, schools and universities get the message out.

> *16 And he shall make all, both little and great, rich and poor, freemen and bondmen, to have a character in their right hand, or on their foreheads.*

> *17 And that no man might buy or sell, but he that hath the character, or the name of the beast, or the number of his name.*

These verses represent the authority over men who voluntarily follow the beast and what he represents as confirmed in chapter 14:9-11. The right hand represents what man does in action through work and the foreheads represent what man believes and thinks.

Verse seventeen, means that the beast controls all aspects of the economy to the degree that the whole world will have to interact with the beast in different ways to survive civilization.

*18 Here is wisdom. He that hath understanding, let him count the number of the beast. For it is the number of a man: and the number of him is six hundred sixty-six.*

The number is apocalyptic which means that it symbolizes or represents something.

Seven is perfection. Six is imperfection.

The number is the perfect antithesis of the number seven which symbolizes perfection.

However, God's last day of creation was on the sixth day as He rested on the seventh. Heaven is the day of peace and rest but hell is eternal chaos and unrest. The beast never rests. He operates on the seventh day because he is stuck in the sixth day.

Even on Sundays, men of the world (the heathens and reprobates) work as they reject the Sabbath. So too, the Devil and his followers continually work against Christ and His Church.

666 is also the weight of gold that came to Solomon every year. (III Kings 10:14)

This gold Solomon kept receiving ties in with men working on the Sabbath to make money.

*"For they that will become rich, fall into temptation, and into the snare of the devil, and into many unprofitable and hurtful desires, which drown men into destruction and perdition.*
*For the desire of money is the root of all evils; which some coveting have erred from the faith, and have entangled themselves in many sorrows."* (I Tim. 6:9-10)

When Jesus told the rich man to obey the Commandments to have eternal life, the rich man said, *"All these I have kept from my youth, what is yet wanting to me?"*

*Jesus saith to him: If thou wilt be perfect, go sell what thou hast, and give to the poor, and thou shalt have treasure in heaven: and come follow me.*

*And when the young man had heard this word, he went away sad: for he had great possessions.*

*Then Jesus said to his disciples: Amen, I say to you, that a rich man shall hardly enter into the kingdom of heaven."* (Matt. 19:20-23)

Christ was pointing out that the rich man did not keep the Commandments for he broke the very first one:

*"Thou shalt not have strange gods before me.*

*Thou shalt not make to thyself a graven thing, nor the likeness of anything that is in heaven above, or in the earth beneath, nor of those things that are in the waters under the earth.*

*Thou shalt not adore them, nor serve them:"* (Ex. 20:3-5)

The rich man makes himself a god adoring and serving himself with a life of money and wealth coming with it worldly power.

Antichrist makes himself out to be a god in the same way.

Chapter 17 reads:

*3 And he took me away in spirit into the desert. And I saw a woman sitting upon a scarlet coloured beast, full of names of blasphemy, having seven heads and ten horns.*

The woman is Rome where the headquarters of Christianity is located. Blasphemy means the beast is in rage against Christ. Rome in a sense also represents the Roman Empire which in turn represents in a broader scope a foreshadowing of a future governmental system such as the New World Order.

*4 And the woman was clothed round about with purple and scarlet, and gilt with gold, and precious stones and pearls, having a golden cup in her hand, full of the abomination and filthiness of her fornication.*

The colors and gems represent royalty, power, and wealth of Rome. They also have a religious significance. Red is a figure of fire and blood, purple is a figure of penitence, and gold represents priestly royalty. The cup full of abomination and filthiness identify Rome's debauchery also spoken about in Chapter 14:8.

*5 And on her forehead a name was written: A mystery; Babylon the great, the mother of the fornications, and the abominations of the earth.*

Babylon is the code word for Rome. St. Peter uses this word to indentify Rome in his epistle. (I Peter 5:13) St. John is quite aware that the headquarters of Christianity is in Rome. The Apocalypse is written for the Church and therefore, he always has the Church in mind when speaking about Babylon. The address is to the seven churches which are real churches in Asia Minor. The churches represent the one Church as all seven churches are of the one Faith. St. John is telling the Church the wrongs within with warnings if not corrected.

*6 And I saw the woman drunk with the blood of the saints, and with the blood of the martyrs of Jesus. And I wondered, when I had seen her, with great admiration.*

The Roman Empire under her cruel emperors executed many Christians. St. John had personally witnessed 10 emperors reign by time he wrote the Apocalypse. Some even interpret the 10 heads of the dragon to represent these 10 emperors.

*7 And the angel said to me: Why dost thou wonder? I will tell thee the mystery of the woman, and of the beast which carrieth her, which hath the seven heads and ten horns.*

*8 The beast, which thou sawest, was, and is not, and shall come up out of the bottomless pit, and go into destruction: and the inhabitants on the earth (whose names are not written in the book of life from the foundation of the world) shall wonder, seeing the beast that was, and is not.*

The dragon is red (Apocalypse 12:3) and according to verse 3 so becomes the beast. With the phrase *"The beast that was, and is not"* in conjunction with the new added color red, marks the time when Satan is released from the pit and possesses the beast *(that was)* in the Old Testament, but *(is not)* possessed after Christ until he is released from the pit.

*9 And here is the understanding that hath wisdom. The seven heads are seven mountains, upon which the woman sitteth, and they are seven kings:*

*10 Five are fallen, one is, and the other is not yet come: and when he is come, he must remain a short time.*

Father George Haydock got this one right in his commentary. The seven here represents the ages of kings. The first five have passed on: Adam to Noah, Noah to Abraham, Abraham to Moses, Moses to David, and David to Christ. Seven means all ages together.

If heads are fallen then the woman could not be sitting on those particular five but the one that is not fallen or the sixth age from the time of Christ to antichrist. The Roman Empire occupied this age during the writing of the Apocalypse. The seventh age is antichrist to the Second Coming of Christ which will be that short time which Satan will have.

*11 And the beast which was, and is not: the same also is the eighth, and is of the seven, and goeth into destruction.*

This was partly explained in verse 8, but the *"eighth"* here represents eternity where Satan resides in hell. The seventh is the time of antichrist.

*12 And the ten horns which thou sawest, are ten kings, who have not yet received a kingdom, but shall receive power as kings one hour after the beast.*

The Greek text has the word *"with"* or *"together"* rather than *"one hour after."* Both ways work. If rendered *"one hour after,"* this would indicate after the pre-possessed beast. If rendered *"with"* then it would be the scarlet beast. Both ways indicate that during the time of antichrist, the whole of nations will be possessed by Satan.

*13 These have one design: and their strength and power they shall deliver to the beast.*

Nations will do all that is possible to destroy Christ as King of Society and Nations. This has been fulfilled to the letter today.

*14 These shall fight with the Lamb, and the Lamb shall overcome them, because he is Lord of lords, and King of kings, and they that are with him are called, and elect, and faithful.*

*15 And he said to me: The waters which thou sawest, where the harlot sitteth, are peoples, and nations, and tongues.*

The harlot sits on the scarlet beast in verse 1 and the heads of the beast in verse 9. Now, St. John says the harlot sits on the waters.

The beast came out of the waters indicating the beast is made of peoples, and nations, and tongues but also the Devil who has taken control of the beast of men. The antichrist is mankind or men of the world possessed by Satan. Christ never spoke about a final antichrist but rather warned of the many false prophets that would come. Antichrist is not one particular man. He is all men not in Christ who has been completely given over to the Devil. He has parts such as leaders, followers, and instigators. The beast becomes scarlet at **1260 days** and after the **1000 years**. Both are symbolic expressions.

*16 And the ten horns which thou sawest in the beast: these shall hate the harlot, and shall make her desolate and naked, and shall eat her flesh, and shall burn her with fire.*

The Greek text has it that both the horns and the beast hate the harlot. Either way, the verse indicates that men of the world hate all authority outside of themselves.

Literally speaking as a secondary interpretation, the nations did hate the Roman Empire which had a certain dominion over them. The empire eventually fell by way of the barbarian invasions.

*17 For God hath given into their hearts to do that which pleaseth him: that they give their kingdom to the beast, till the words of God be fulfilled.*

God allowed the restraining angel to free Satan one last time that Christ's defeat of the Devil will manifest the Glory of God.

*18 And the woman which thou sawest, is the great city, which hath kingdom over the kings of the earth.*

Chapter 18 begins where chapter 17 leaves off. St. John will be knocking out two birds with one stone here. By referencing Rome, the first thing anyone thinks of in St. John's future is the Church. So it is with St John who is prophesying the status of the future Church within a new empire that Rome foreshadowed; the New World Order.

*1 And after these things, I saw another angel come down from heaven, having great power: and the earth was enlightened with his glory.*

*2 And he cried out with a strong voice, saying: Babylon the great is fallen, is fallen; and is become the habitation of devils, and the hold of every unclean spirit, and the hold of every unclean and hateful bird:*

Rome was apparently not inhabited with demons before it fell and it fell as a harlot! The reason being was the institutional Church was alive within her keeping hell at bay.

The gates of hell shall not prevail against the Church but as St. John warns in chapter 2, those gates may prevail against parts of the Church. In fact, by stating that Rome is now inhabited by devils, he is implying that the church at Rome is gone!

The Church is what has fallen because she lost her faith due to the pressure of hell around her. In other words, she gave in and apostatized. This is the end of the 1260 days and when the antichrist will soon reign.

St. John's seeing the future confirms what St. Paul spoke about to the Thessalonians about a great falling away or apostasy.

The church at Rome falls just as the Roman Empire fell; by way of corruption within and pressure from the outside.

However, the apostate church justifies it all as the will of God by the authority that He gave the Church which they claim (falsely) is theirs.

> *3 Because all nations have drunk of the wine of the wrath of her fornication; and the kings of the earth have committed fornication with her; and the merchants of the earth have been made rich by the power of her delicacies.*

The RSV states, *"for all nations have drunk the wine of her impure passion, and the kings of the earth have committed fornication with her, and the merchants of the earth have grown rich with the wealth of her wantonness."*

The verse is saying that the world relished in the heresy that the church at Rome inherited from the world.

Catholics who apostatize with the church at Rome will be fornicating (hobnobbing with false religions and their practices) as well since they will have abandoned the true Faith.

Without the condemnations from the old and true Roman Church, the rest of the world takes advantage of the situation approving what was once considered erroneous.

The Roman Empire went the same route.

*4 And I heard another voice from heaven, saying: Go out from her, my people; that you be not partakers of her sins, and that you receive not of her plagues.*

This is a clear warning to steer clear from the apostasy. Our Lord gave the same warning in (Matt. 24:16-21).

To go out from implies that God's people were in and followed her but now have to leave and no longer follow her.

Continuing down to verses 7 and 8, St. John gives us an accurate view of the church at Rome today.

*7 As much as she hath glorified herself, and lived in delicacies, so much torment and sorrow give ye to her; because she saith in her heart: I sit a queen, and am no widow; and sorrow I shall not see.*

*8 Therefore shall her plagues come in one day, death, and mourning, and famine, and she shall be burnt with the fire; because God is strong, who shall judge her.*

The church at Rome glorifies in the new understanding of herself and her role in the world. She claims to be a queen and no widow meaning she has a husband who is a king. Yet, she fornicates making her an adulteress while thinking she'll be alright since her husband is the King who will forgive her regardless.

The King is Christ and His Bride is the Church.

Today, the church at Rome claims to be *the* Church and yet fools around with false religions as in the Assisi Events, dictators, and even Communists as with the Soviets and Chinese.

However, Christ won't forgive the presumptuous or those who feign a love for Christ and the Church. In the end, He will send her straight to hell.

*9 And the kings of the earth, who have committed fornication, and lived in delicacies with her, shall weep, and bewail themselves over her, when they shall see the smoke of her burning:*

The other nations who are filled with the followers of the church at Rome will also be in hell and they will weep, and bewail themselves regretting the fornication they had with her.

*10 Standing afar off for fear of her torments, saying: Alas! alas! that great city Babylon, that mighty city: for in one hour is thy judgment come.*

The judgment on the church at Rome will be much more severe than the rest of the world, therefore will be much deeper in hell. The world in hell will see the torments of 'the one given so much' but spurned what she had. The great city that falls is Rome and its Empire. So also, the church at Rome will fall.

The next verses are explaining the losses suffered in hell which the world enjoyed with the harlot.

*21 And a mighty angel took up a stone, as it were a great millstone, and cast it into the sea, saying: With such violence as this shall Babylon, that great city, be thrown down, and shall be found no more at all.*

Millstone around the neck and cast into sea is the phrase used by Jesus as a punishment for those who lead children astray. (Matt. 18:6, Mk. 9:42, Luke 17:2)

The children of God were led astray by the church at Rome as the church was led astray by the New World Order (the new Roman Empire).

*22 And the voice of harpers, and of musicians, and of them that play on the pipe, and on the trumpet, shall no more be heard at all in thee; and no craftsman of any art whatsoever shall be found any more at all in thee; and the sound of the mill shall be heard no more at all in thee;*

Hell is eternal and the rest of the world in hell with the woman shall never again taste the goodness God had given them in their time in the world. All their riches have passed away.

*"Heaven and earth shall pass away."* (Matt. 24:35, Luke 21:33)

*"And they that use this world, as if they used it not: for the fashion of this world passeth away."* (I Cor. 7:31)

The description given by St. John mirrors that what St. Peter told the Church:

*"But the day of the Lord shall come as a thief, in which the heavens shall pass away with great violence, and the elements shall be melted with heat, and the earth and the works which are in it, shall be burnt up."* (II Peter 3:10)

*23 And the light of the lamp shall shine no more at all in thee; and the voice of the bridegroom and the bride shall be heard no more at all in thee: for thy merchants were the great men of the earth, for all nations have been deceived by thy enchantments.*

St. John is reemphasizing the church at Rome with this verse. The lamp in the sanctuary of each Catholic Church symbolizes the light of Christ present in the Eucharist.

The Bridegroom is Christ and His grace will be absent in the woman, the harlot, the church at Rome. The bride is the Church clearly referencing the fact that the church at Rome is not the Catholic Church since she apostatized.

The nations deceived were filled with all those followers of the church at Rome who failed in heeding the word of Jesus to flee to the mountains.

## The Abomination

During the time of Christ, the Hebrews would go to the Temple to make sacrifices fulfilling the Mosaic Law.

Christ who is the fulfillment of the Law gives Israel and the world a New Covenant in His Blood. With this New Covenant, animal sacrifices will no longer apply but rather the representation of Christ's own sacrifice using bread and wine.

*"1 For the law having a shadow of the good things to come, not the very image of the things; by the selfsame sacrifices which they offer continually every year, can never make the comers thereunto perfect:*

*2 For then they would have ceased to be offered: because the worshippers once cleansed should have no conscience of sin any longer:*

*3 But in them there is made a commemoration of sins every year.*

*4 For it is impossible that with the blood of oxen and goats sin should be taken away.*

*5 Wherefore when he cometh into the world, he saith: Sacrifice and oblation thou wouldest not: but a body thou hast fitted to me:*

*6 Holocausts for sin did not please thee.*

*7 Then said I: Behold I come: in the head of the book it is written of me: that I should do thy will, O God.*

*8 In saying before, Sacrifices, and oblations, and holocausts for sin thou wouldest not, neither are they pleasing to thee, which are offered according to the law.*

*9 Then said I: Behold, I come to do thy will, O God: he taketh away the first, that he may establish that which followeth.*

*10 In the which will, we are sanctified by the oblation of the body of Jesus Christ once.*

*11 And every priest indeed standeth daily ministering, and often offering the same sacrifices, which can never take away sins.*

*12 But this man offering one sacrifice for sins, forever sitteth on the right hand of God,*

*13 From henceforth expecting, until his enemies be made his footstool.*

*14 For by one oblation he hath perfected for ever them that are sanctified.*

*15 And the Holy Ghost also doth testify this to us. For after that he said:*

*16 And this is the testament which I will make unto them after those days, saith the Lord. I will give my laws in their hearts, and on their minds will I write them:*

*17 And their sins and iniquities I will remember no more."* (Hebrews 10:1-17)

When Jesus warns His people to flee the coming abomination, they would immediately think of the abomination found in the book of Maccabees and understood it to mean a false sacrifice would take place in the Temple. However, the children of Israel will not understand until after Pentecost that Christ meant that the present animal sacrifices would be the abomination of desolation in rejection of the sacrifice of Christ's own Body and Blood.

*"When therefore you shall see the abomination of desolation, which was spoken of by Daniel the prophet, standing in the holy place: he that readeth let him understand."* (The Holy Gospel of Jesus Christ, According to St. Matthew 24:15 and St. Mark 13:14)

This was the answer Christ gave after being asked by one of his disciples, *"what shall be the sign of thy coming and of the consummation of the world?"* (Matt 24:3)

Later, Christ said, *"But of that day and hour no one knoweth."* (Matt 24:36), *"Watch ye therefore, because ye know not what hour your Lord will come."* (Matt 24:42)

Christ is simply saying that we can't know precisely when He will come again, but that we must be prepared especially during certain events, which will be taking place at that time. In other words, He is hinting when it will happen.

God gives us other hints as in (II Thessalonians 2:3). A great apostasy and the revealing of the man of sin or antichrist will be at the same general time of Christ's Second Coming.

This study has already demonstrated the fulfillment of the prophecies of the great apostasy and the antichrist.

So when we see the next sign which is the abomination of desolation standing in the holy place foretold by Daniel, Christ commands us to flee. (Matt. 24:15, Mark 13:14)

The abomination is a false worship service with a false sacrifice and offering. When the true sacrifice and offering ceases due to the false sacrifice, this is the desolation, thus we have the abomination of desolation.

Throughout history, out from the Catholic Church false worship services with false sacrifices have taken place with those apostasies mentioned on page 53.

### The prophecies of Daniel

*"And he shall confirm the covenant with many, in one week: and in the half of the week the victim and the sacrifice shall fail: and there shall be in the temple the abomination of desolation: and the desolation shall continue even to the consummation, and to the end."* (Daniel 9:27)

He refers to Christ as the previous verses name Him. One week refers to the last days. Half of the week refers to a time after the beginning of the last days.

*"And arms shall stand on his part, and they shall defile the sanctuary of strength, and shall take away the continual sacrifice: and they shall place there the abomination unto desolation."* (Daniel 11:31)

Daniel is prophesying the abomination of desolation of Antiochus IV Epiphanes who set up his idol of Jupiter for three and half years. This abomination is but a foreshadowing of the final abomination.

*"And from the time when the continual sacrifice shall be taken away, and the abomination unto desolation shall be set up, there shall be a thousand two hundred ninety days.*
*Blessed is he that waiteth and cometh unto a thousand three hundred thirty-five days.*
*But go thou thy ways until the time appointed: and thou shalt rest, and stand in thy lot unto the end of the days."* (Daniel 12:11-13)

Daniel who used the foreshadowing of Antiochus is now speaking about the final abomination.

When the abomination takes place, antichrist must already be in the world. His time comes after the 1260 days and the abomination comes after the 1290 days. The time of 1290 days is symbolic meaning sometime shortly before the return of Christ.

The prophet Malachi speaks of the continual sacrifice, *"For from the rising of the sun even to the going down, my name is great among the Gentiles, and in every place there is sacrifice, and there is offered to my name a clean oblation: for my name is great among the Gentile, saith the Lord of hosts."* (Mal. 1:11)

Daniel's continual sacrifice was a reference to the Old Covenant sacrifices in the Temple. Christ put an end to it with His own sacrifice. The animal sacrifices that were continued by the apostate Jews were not true sacrifices to God. Daniel's 1290 days begin with Christ and not the destruction of the temple in 70 AD.

Christ's sacrifice found at the Holy Mass was the one Malachi was referring to and this sacrifice will cease for a period (*half of the week*) before the end of time as foretold in (Daniel 9:27).

The first abomination of desolation prophesied by Daniel takes place in the book of Machabees (Maccabees).

Under the reign of Antiochus IV Epiphanes in 175 BC, the abomination of desolation takes place in the Holy Temple. To make his abomination of desolation, Antiochus erects a second altar against the first altar in (I Macc. 1:57-62).

As part of the abomination of Antiochus, women were involved in the worship service along with other unlawful acts, and the solemn days of the fathers were not observed (II Macc. 6:4).

The second abomination of desolation took place immediately after the death of our Lord when the Jews who rejected Him kept offering animal sacrifices in the temple of Jerusalem until approximately 40 to 41 years later when the Gentiles completely destroyed the Temple in 70 AD.

The third and final abomination of desolation is taking place now as will be demonstrated in relation to the first two major abominations of history.

The novus ordo missae of Paul VI is the abomination foretold by the prophet Daniel and the abomination Christ warns his followers to flee from.

The novus ordo missae or new mass made the true sacrifice (Roman Mass of Popes Sts. Pius V and X) desolate.

This new mass also has a second altar against the first, with women serving in the sanctuary as they perform unlawful acts of dancing, speaking, and distributing communion.

The novus ordo calendar does not observe the solemn days of the Fathers and leaves out the very verses of (Matt. 24), which foretells of the great abomination of desolation.

In the next chapter, the first abomination of Antiochus will be presented as foreshadowing the modern day abomination of the new Roman church.

The similarities are staggering!

# The Abominations between Antiochus and Paul VI

### I Maccabees Chapter 1 (RSV CE):

*20 After subduing Egypt, Antiochus returned in the one hundred and forty-third year. He went up against Israel and came to Jerusalem with a strong force.*

(Paul VI went up against the New Israel (Church) with a strong force of modernist prelates.)

*21 He arrogantly entered the sanctuary and took the golden altar, the lampstand for the light, and all its utensils.*

(The lampstand indicating the real substantial presence of our Lord in the Tabernacle has been removed in many churches.)

*22 He took also the table for the bread of the Presence, the cups for drink offerings, the bowls, the golden censers, the curtain, the crowns, and the gold decoration on the front of the temple; he stripped it all off.*

(The altars have been removed and replaced with tables.)

*23 He took the silver and the gold, and the costly vessels; he took also the hidden treasures which he found.*

(The costly vessels or chalices are now cheap glassware and the hidden treasures or Tabernacles have been taken to back rooms.)

*43 All the Gentiles accepted the command of the king. Many even from Israel gladly adopted his religion; they sacrificed to idols and profaned the sabbath.*

(Nearly the whole Catholic world accepted Vatican 2 and the new mass from Paul VI, and the new idols are self, man's rights, money, and power.)

*44 And the king sent letters by messengers to Jerusalem and the cities of Judah; he directed them to follow customs strange to the land,*
*45 to forbid burnt offerings and sacrifices and drink offerings in the sanctuary, to profane sabbaths and feasts,*

(The Roman Mass was forbidden, and feast days abolished.)

*46 to defile the sanctuary and the priests,*
*47 to build altars and sacred precincts and shrines for idols, to sacrifice swine and unclean animals,*

(Sanctuaries have been revamped; priests persecuted, and new table altars have been placed while sharing with Protestant services. Bread and wine rather than the Body and Blood of Christ.)

*48 and to leave their sons uncircumcised. They were to make themselves abominable by everything unclean and profane,*
*49 so that they should forget the law and change all the ordinances.*

(The Roman Mass was eliminated with all the great feasts and replaced by the new laws of modernists. The many days of penitential fasting and abstaining are completely eliminated by Rome.)

*50 "And whoever does not obey the command of the king shall die."*

(Excommunication was exacted on those who openly kept the historic Catholic Faith.)

*51 In such words he wrote to his whole kingdom. And he appointed inspectors over all the people and commanded the cities of Judah to offer sacrifice, city by city.*
*52 Many of the people, everyone who forsook the law, joined them, and they did evil in the land;*
*53 they drove Israel into hiding in every place of refuge they had.*
*54 Now on the fifteenth day of Chislev, in the one hundred and forty-fifth year, they erected a desolating sacrilege upon the altar of burnt offering. They also built altars in the surrounding cities of Judah,*
*59 And on the twenty-fifth day of the month they offered sacrifice on the altar which was upon the altar of burnt offering.*

(The underground Catholic Church has been driven away and persecuted by the new modernist religion of Rome.)

II Macc. 6:4: *"...And women thrust themselves of their own accord into the holy places, and brought in things that were not lawful. The altar was also filled with unlawful things, which were forbidden by the laws. And neither were...the solemn days of the fathers observed..."*

(Women are all over the sanctuary as altar servers, lectors, dancers, and as acolytes.)

The 1962 Missal of John XXIII is also in union with modernist Rome.

Christ commands us to flee from the abomination, not continue some type of true sacrifice alongside of the Abomination so that it no longer makes desolate.

The 62' mass begins with disobedience to Christ and requires that the abomination be accepted as a true sacrificial offering.

# The New Mass of Paul VI

In 1969, Paul VI promulgated the second version of the new mass, which was fabricated by a high-ranking Vatican Official who was a Freemason along with the aid of six Protestants and two "*Catholics.*" (*The Eternal War*, Tape 3. *The Keys of the Kingdom* – Fr. Malachi Martin, interviewed by Bernard Janzen, Triumph Communications)

Paul VI publicly thanked them for their assistance in re-editing in a new manner liturgical texts ... so that the *lex orandi* (the law of prayer) conformed better with the *lex credendi* (the law of belief). (Fr. Rama Coomaraswamy, *The Problems with the New Mass*, TAN Books p. 24.)

This new mass is very evil not only in how it was drawn up but also in the intention of each change.

*"Evil thoughts are an abomination to the Lord"* (Book of Proverbs 15:26) and evil thoughts are most certainly on the minds of John XXIII, who knowingly prepared the way of the new mass with his 1962 missal, and Paul VI, following John's lead, took it to the next level with the new modernist mass.

The novus ordo missae had changed from the Roman Mass into what resembled both Luther's Mass and the Anglican Mass.

Jean Guitton, a distinguished French writer as well as the great friend and confidant of Paul VI, described Paul's *"intention with regard to the liturgy... (which) was to reform the Catholic liturgy in such a way that it should almost coincide with the Protestant liturgy...beyond the Council of Trent, (and) closer to the Protestant Lord's Supper...(making) less room for all that some would call 'magic,' (namely) ...transubstantial consecration, and for all what is of the Catholic Faith:' ...there was with Paul VI an ecumenical intention to remove...what was too Catholic, in the traditional sense, in the Mass, and, I repeat, to get the Catholic*

*Mass closer to the Calvinist mass."* (Broadcast December 19, 1993 by Radio-Courtoisie, Paris.)

The altering of the mass comes from the implementation of Vatican 2's *Sacrosanctum Concilium.*

*SC # 34:* "*The rites should radiate a rich simplicity; they should be brief and lucid, avoiding pointless repetitions; they should be intelligible for the people, and should not in general require much explanation.*"

*SC # 50:* "*Therefore the rites, in a way that carefully preserves what really matters, should become simpler. Duplications which have come in over the course of time should be discontinued, as should the less useful accretions.*"

However, these two propositions contradict Pope Pius VI, *Auctorem fidei,* Aug. 28. 1794, # 33:

"*The proposition of the synod by which it shows itself eager to remove the cause through which, in part, there has been induced a forgetfulness of the principles relating to the order of the liturgy, 'by recalling it (the liturgy) to a greater simplicity of rites, by expressing it in the vernacular language, by uttering it in a loud voice...'*" – *Condemned as rash, offensive to pious ears, insulting to the Church, favorable to the charges of heretics against it.*

*SC # 30:* "*In order to encourage their taking an active share, acclamations for the people, together with responses, psalmody, antiphons and hymns, should be developed, as well as actions, movements and bodily self-expression.*"

*SC # 37:* "*... (the Church) cultivates and encourages the gifts and endowments of mind and heart possessed by various races in peoples... Indeed, it sometimes allows them into the liturgy itself, provided they are consistent with the thinking behind the true spirit of the liturgy.*"

*SC # 40:* *"However, in some places or in some situations, there may arise a pressing need for a more radical adaptation of the liturgy."*

*SC # 40.1: "The competent local Church authority should carefully and conscientiously consider, in this regard, which elements from the traditions and particular talents of individual peoples can be brought into divine worship. Adaptations which are adjudged useful or necessary should be proposed to the apostolic see, and introduced with its consent."*

Pope St. Pius X understood and condemned this line of thinking as modernist.

Pope St. Pius X, *Pascendi Dominici Gregis* (# 26), Sept. 8, 1907, On the Worship of Modernists: *"The chief stimulus in the domain of worship consists in the need of adapting itself to the uses and customs of peoples, as well as the need of availing itself of the value which certain acts have acquired by long usage."*

Paul VI rejected this condemnation as Ratzinger would later say for being *"obsolete."*

# What makes the New Mass the Abomination

The church at Rome has given into the world's desire to be God and so raised the dignity of man to the level of God. The next step is to create a liturgy or new worship service to reflect this fact.

The new mass is directed towards man and God rather than God alone.

The focus is on the participation of man rather than the priest acting *in persona Christi*.

This replacement of man and God rather than to God alone is an abomination in and of itself.

The second beast represents false religion which makes the world worship itself.

Now that man's dignity is raised to the level of God, Christ's words at the Consecration will be changed so as to include all men rather than believers only.

The words Christ used were *"for many"* not *"for all."*

According to the new religion of Vatican 2, since man is so dignified that all things on earth should be related to man as their center and crown, and his exceptional dignity which gives man superiority over everything and whose rights are universal and inviolable, who is to be loved by all on the same plane as God, then the Eucharist should be for all men.

However, this is all absolutely contrary to historic Christianity.

According to the infallible decree of Pope Eugene IV, at the Council of Florence in Session 8, on Nov. 22, 1439, *"Exultate Deo,"* several things must be present for a Mass to be valid.

*"All these sacraments are made up of three elements: namely, things as the matter, words as the form, and the person of the minister who confers the sacrament with the intention of doing what the Church does. If any of these is lacking, the sacrament is not effected."* (*Decrees of the Ecumenical Councils*, Georgetown Univ. Press, Vol. 1, p. 542; Denzinger, *The Sources of Catholic Dogma*, no. 695)

The words of the 'form' used at the Consecration over the Chalice at the new mass are: *"This is the cup of my Blood...which will be shed for you and for all so that sins may be forgiven."*

For this reason, the incorrect 'form' of the Consecration of the new mass is invalid. Therefore, a false worship ceremony is taking place where it should not, and thus you have an abomination.

*"For every mocker is an abomination to the Lord."* (Book of Proverbs 3:32)

The new mass mocks the Roman Mass of Pope St. Pius V as the priests mock our Lord's words.

*"Lying lips are an abomination to the Lord."* (Book of Proverbs 12:22)

The priests are lying when they state at the Consecration that our Lord says *"for all."*

*"The way of the wicked is an abomination to the Lord."* (Book of Proverbs 15:9)

Falsifying our Lord's words at the most solemn moment in time, is the most wicked of ways.

Some have argued that *"all"* and *"many"* can be used interchangeably as sometimes happens in Scripture. Therefore, *"all"* best shows the meaning of what "many" really means.

Even the Offertory says, *"We offer unto Thee, O Lord, the chalice of salvation, humbly begging of Thy mercy that it may arise before Thy divine majesty with a pleasing fragrance, for our salvation and that of all the world. Amen."*

It is true that the words are juxtaposed in Scripture at times without changing the meaning. However, the Catechism of the Council of Trent promulgated by Pope St. Pius V under St. Charles Borromeo clearly refutes the rest of this objection.

It states:

*On the Form of the Eucharist:*

*"The additional words for you and for many, are taken, some from Matthew, some from Luke, but were joined together by the Catholic Church under the guidance of the Spirit of God. They serve to declare the fruit and advantage of His Passion. For if we look to its value, we must confess that the Redeemer shed His Blood for the salvation of all; but if we look to the fruit which mankind has received from it, we shall easily find that it pertains not unto all, but to many of the human race. When therefore (our Lord) said: For you, He meant either those who were present, or those chosen from among the Jewish people, such as were, with the exception of Judas, the disciples with whom He was speaking. When He added, And for many, He wished to be understood to mean the remainder of the elect from among the Jews and Gentiles. With reason, therefore, were the words 'for all' no used, as in this place the fruits of the Passion are alone spoken of, and to the elect only did His Passion bring the fruit of salvation."* (*The Catechism of the Council of Trent*, TAN Books, 1982, p. 227.)

Though both words are at times used interchangeably in Scripture, the official Catechism of the Council of Trent, the Church says specifically *"for all"* renders a different meaning than *"many."*

Pope Benedict XIV (1740-1758) discussed this issue and stated that this teaching "explains correctly" Christ's use of *"for many,"* as opposed to *"for all"* (*De Sacrosanctae Missae Sacrificio*).

The Catechism is actually addressing the error of previous heretics who wanted the words changed back in the 16th century.

The simple fact is the word all cannot always be used in place of the word many.

We know Christ would not use hyperbole in the most sacred moment in history. He used the word many to refer to only the Faithful and not to all of humanity as the Catechism explains.

The great 18th century theologian Fr. Martinus von Cochem O.S.F wrote in his book *"The Holy Sacrifice of the Mass Explained"* p. 111:

*"Consequently, the Precious Blood of Christ is in real fact shed in the Mass "for you and for many"; that is, for you who are attending and attentive, and for the many who are absent; for those who assisting if they could do so and who therefore desire a memento in it. These are the "many" for the remission of whose sins Christ's Blood is shed in the Mass."*

As for the Offertory, it is not Christ but the Faithful who is offering the Chalice for all of humanity. The note in some Roman Missals on this part of the Offertory says, *"We pray "for our salvation," and yes, "and that of all the world."* Of course, the Faithful would pray and ask for all of the world to come to the truth and receive Communion before they die, but it does not follow that Christ would actually give the Chalice of His Blood to all of the world.

It is ludicrous to say the Offertory proves the 'form' should also mean for all.

A second objection in justifying the word "all" is that the essential part of the 'form' is: *"This is my Body, and This is my Blood."* Therefore, the words *"all"* and *"many"* do not matter.

This argument is saying that once the priest says, *"For this is the Chalice of My Blood"* the wine is changed into the Blood of Christ regardless to what the priest says later in the 'form.' This explanation is completely unfounded.

First, the Council of Florence has pronounced as de fide the whole 'form' is what actuates the change in substance and not just parts of the 'form.'

**Pope St. Pius V**

153

Pope St. Pius V said in *"De Defectibus"* Chapter 5, Part 1:

*"The words of Consecration, which are the form of this sacrament, are these: FOR THIS IS MY BODY. AND: FOR THIS IS THE CHALICE OF MY BLOOD, OF THE NEW AND ETERNAL TESTAMENT: THE MYSTERY OF FAITH, WHICH SHALL BE SHED FOR YOU AND FOR MANY UNTO THE REMISSION OF SINS. Now if one were to remove, or change anything in the form of the consecration of the body and blood, and in that very change of words the [NEW] wording would fail to mean the same thing, he would not consecrate the sacrament."*

Notice that St. Pius V did not say that one could not remove, or change anything in the 'form' but one could not remove, or change anything, which would give it a different meaning. This is a very crucial distinction. Throughout history, there have been changes with variants and omissions but the proper meaning stayed intact.

Pope St. Pius V was reiterating what Pope Eugene IV at the Council of Florence stated in Session 11, Feb 1442:

*"However, since no explanation was given in the aforesaid decree of the Armenians in respect to the form of words which the holy Roman Church, relying on the teaching and authority of the apostles Peter and Paul, has always been wont to use in the consecration of the Lord's Body and Blood, we concluded that it should be inserted in this present text. It uses this form of words in the consecration of the Lord's Body: FOR THIS IS MY BODY. And of His blood: FOR THIS IS THE CHALICE OF MY BLOOD, OF THE NEW AND ETERNAL TESTAMENT: THE MYSTERY OF FAITH, WHICH SHALL BE SHED FOR YOU AND FOR MANY UNTO THE REMISSION OF SINS."* (*Decrees of the Ecumenical Councils*, Vol. 1, p. 581).

The Catechism promulgated by Pope St. Pius V says that *"all"* does not mean the same thing as *"many."* This pope also stated, *"in that very change of words the new wording would fail to mean the same thing, he would not consecrate the sacrament."*

St. Alphonsus De Liguori had this to say on the 'form':

*"The words pro vobis et pro multis (for you and for many) are used to distinguish the virtue of the Blood of Christ from its fruits: for the Blood of Our Savior is of sufficient value to save all men **but its fruits are applied only to a certain number and not to all**, and this is their own fault... This is the explanation of St. Thomas, as quoted by [Pope] Benedict XIV."* (St. Alphonsus De Liguori, *Treatise on The Holy Eucharist,* Redemptorist Fathers, 1934, p. 44)

The consecration takes place after the whole 'form' is recited and not just parts of it.

To demonstrate this point: Let's suppose over the Chalice the priest said only, *"For this is the Chalice of My Blood...but only as a symbol and not actually."*

Would you really argue the Blood of Christ was actually made present after this particular form?

Of course not, because the form had words which changed the overall meaning and because the added words demonstrated the wrong intention of the priest.

This proves the wine does not change immediately after those "essential" words: *"For this is the Chalice of My Blood"* precisely because the de fide position is the **WHOLE FORM** is what actuates the change in substance and not just parts of it.

Interesting enough, the documents *Quo Primum* and *De Defectibus* were found in the front of all Altar Missals and placed in the *Missale Romanum* in 1572. In 1969, ICEL (Committee on English in the Liturgy) deleted them in the new versions.

*Quo Primum* written by St. Pope Pius V on July 14, 1570 stated:

*"It shall be unlawful henceforth and forever throughout the Christian world to sing or to read Masses according to any formula other than this Missal published by us...This present Constitution can never be revoked or modified, but shall forever remain valid and have the force of Law . . . And if, nevertheless, anyone would ever dare attempt any action contrary to this Order of ours, handed down for all times, let him know that he has incurred the wrath of Almighty God, and the Blessed Apostles Peter and Paul."*

Why would these important documents be omitted unless there was a sinister agenda to do away with the Tradition of the Church?

Another problem with this objection is the signifying effect of the sacrament is erroneous or would be missing altogether in its wording.

Pope Leo XIII in his 1896 document *Apostolicae Curae* concerning the invalidity of the Anglican Orders states:

*"All know that the Sacraments of the New Law, as sensible and efficient signs of invisible grace, must both signify the grace which they effect and effect the grace which they signify.... That form cannot be considered apt or sufficient for a Sacrament which omits that which it must essentially signify."*

Even though Pope Leo XIII was speaking about the sacrament of Holy Orders, the principle applies to all sacraments. This would apply especially to the Eucharist for this is the greatest and source of all the sacraments.

It is necessary for the words *"for many unto the remission of sins"* to be correct and not to be omitted because they form part of the FORM.

If the words are not the same as Christ's words and the new words mean something different, two parts necessary for a valid Mass are missing: The Form, because the words are different having with it a different meaning and the Intention of the Church because something else was intended as the very words indicate.

Pope Leo XIII declared the Holy Orders of the Anglican Church invalid due to a defective 'form.' The new rite of Ordination in the modernist so-called Catholic Church mirrors that of the Anglican Church and with the very same deficiencies. This means the new rite of Ordination in the church at Rome is also invalid.

An invalid priesthood would necessarily invalidate the Eucharist. Thus, three necessary parts are missing to make a valid mass.

Even a true pope is limited in his authority. He cannot officially change the words of Christ anymore than he could change the matter, which Christ used. In other words, the pope could not change bread and wine to pretzels and beer as the heretic Thomas Munzer did in the 16th century.

If a true pope ever did try to do such a thing, he would ipso facto cease to be pope, since it is impossible for a true pope to command an erroneous, harmful, or evil universal discipline.

The word *"all"* by itself is not found in the Ancient Eastern Rites. Although an ancient anaphora might state, *"for all that believes"* or *"all the true faithful."* Of course, this means the same thing as *"many."*

The fact is the Aramaic word does not have as its meaning *"for all."* Never in history or in Scripture do we see this in the Consecration. According to Fr. Malachi Martin, doctor and the premier expert in ancient Semitic Languages, states that there are two Aramaic words for *"all"* and two for *"many."* (*The Eternal War*, Tape 3. *The Keys of the Kingdom* – Fr. Malachi Martin, interviewed by Bernard Janzen, Triumph Communications)

Another objection sometimes used to justify the change is the host cannot change without the Chalice. Therefore, if the host changes, the wine must also change since you can't have half of a sacrament.

However, the Host alone is not just half of the sacrament. The whole Christ is present in the consecrated Host: Body, Blood, Soul, and Divinity.

At every Holy Mass, presuming all the elements are present, the host will change before the Chalice since Catholics adore the Host before the second part of the Consecration takes place.

If a valid priest honestly forgets to consecrate the wine in the Chalice, the Host would still remain valid with Christ fully present, if it did not, then Christ would be present one moment and cease being present a moment later. The only other possibility would be that Christ would have never been present in the host thus rendering adoration to a piece of ordinary bread by the Faithful a moment earlier.

Though the Church has never defined what would happen in either scenario, the argument does not follow that the Chalice must be valid. It could only support the possibility that Christ is not present in the host as well.

Without the correct intention in the second part of the Consecration, the host would also not transubstantiate precisely because there was never the correct intention in the beginning.

Another very interesting objection is used to justify the word *"all"* is:

Based on the Scriptural usage, the replacement of *"many"* with "all" does not represent a material change in the consecration formula, for both *"many"* and *"all"* can be either inclusive or exclusive. Whether the inclusive or exclusive meaning is intended in (Matthew 26:28 and Mark 14:24) is neither specified by Scripture nor taught in any papal or conciliar dogma. Yet we must add that even in its most inclusive sense, the Scriptural usage of "all" does not mean that every person in the world *will be* saved, but only that every person has the *opportunity* to be saved.

However, regardless of the wording whether *"many"* or *"all,"* if the intention of either word is inclusive, then the wrong intention would be present because it is not referring to who or who is not going to be saved.

The 'form' is not merely referring to every person who has an opportunity to be saved because all of mankind has the opportunity to be saved.

The Chalice is offered only to those who believe. The Faithful are the fruits of Christ's redemption.

The assumption is not made whether the Faithful will remain faithful to the end, just as the fruits may not remain good until harvest.

This is the key. It doesn't matter whether the ones receiving the Cup will be saved or not because the potentiality of salvation of the soul is based on the endurance of the individual.

This is why the Eucharist is given to the believers. The Eucharist is our daily bread to help keep us spiritually alive and healthy and to give us strength.

Thus, the statement that said, "...for both *"many"* and *"all"* can be either inclusive or exclusive... Whether the inclusive or exclusive meaning is intended in (Matthew 26:28 and Mark 14:24) is neither specified by Scripture," is denied in the Catechism of the Council of Trent and by St. Alphonsus and Scripture itself.

It would be the height of arrogance, not to mention outright heretical, to argue against the Holy Scriptures, the Catechism of Trent and St. Alphonsus and say anyone whosoever can receive from the Chalice and that it could be inclusive.

For it is and has always has been only for those who believe which are Catholics, thus making this understanding a dogma precisely because it is in Scripture itself, and confirmed by the consistent and unambiguous writings of Pope St. Pius V, St. Charles Borremeo, and St. Alphonsus De Liguori.

*"For anyone who eats and drinks without discerning the body eats and drinks judgment upon himself."*(First Letter to the Corinthians 11:29)

This is dogma!

Lastly, it is said that Pope St. Pius V in *De Defectibus* tells us exactly what the *"intention"* required to consecrate the sacrament must be. And that intention has absolutely nothing to do with whether the priest intends to share the fruits of the Lord's blood with *"many"* or "all" men. In paragraph 23 of the document, Pope Pius V states:

*"The intention of consecrating is required."*

While it is true that the intention of consecration is required, the question is about the requirement of consecrating.

The intention of consecration lies in the 'form,' which is why it is in the 'form.' Pope St. Pius V said that if you change the 'form' to mean something different such as consecrating it for all mankind, then you would have the wrong intention. It wouldn't be in the 'form' if the intention were not going to be a part of it.

The intention is consecrating, but that doesn't mean merely changing the substance without the purpose of changing it. This is why all the words matter as St. Thomas and St. Alphonsus affirmed.

The Council of Florence has given us the de fide position; the whole 'form' is what changes the substance.

Again, the consecration requires the intent to change the wine and its purpose if that purpose is part of the 'form.'

Rome hates Christ and His words and intentions.

The new mass as a whole is profoundly non-Catholic, non-historical, and non-biblical and that is the way it was meant to be according to those who drew it up.

Amazingly, the 'liturgy of the word' in the new mass will quote Christ saying *"for many"* and the priest's duty is to explain the 'liturgy of the word' in his homily. A few minutes later, the priest uses the words "for all" during the Consecration right after everyone just heard Christ saying it is not for all but for the many, and nobody is the wiser.

The modernist church just keeps up the mockery and sacrilege.

Modernist Masonic Rome has admitted that *"all"* is a bad translation but only to counter people like this author as they keep their faithful confused and lost on the subject.

The fact is *"all"* is more than just a mere bad translation, it is a harmful one which is impossible for the true Catholic Church to do according to the solemn teachings of at least five popes.

It should be noted, the Council of Trent in the 7th Session, Canon 13 said: *"If anyone says that the received and approved rites of the Catholic Church, customarily used in the solemn administration of the Sacrament, can be despise or can be freely omitted by the ministers without sin, or can be changed into other new rites by any pastor in the Church whomsoever, let him be anathema"*

The key phrases are *"other new rites...by any pastor whomsoever."*

This binds all future popes. PERIOD!

Again, in the Ancient or Roman Rite, there is an Altar, and in its rubrics, there is an offering of Christ's Body and Blood.

In the new rite, there is a table and in its rubrics, there is an offering of bread and wine.

The abomination of desolation found in the book of Maccabees had two altars. One was placed over the other just as in today's so-called Catholic Church. This is quite a coincidence. The Old Testament abomination also had women serving in the sanctuary. (II Maccabees 6:4)

Again, Jesus spoke of a future abomination of desolation in (Matthew 24:15), *"So when you see the desolating sacrilege spoken of by the prophet Daniel, standing in the holy place (let the reader understand)..."*

This is the last Gospel reading of the liturgical year on the Roman calendar, yet this verse is not found in all of the Gospel readings throughout the entire year in the new liturgical (new mass) calendar. Why?

Christ was referring to the new mass and Masonic Rome knows it.

The new mass should be solemnly condemned with all our power for it does not fit in the Catholic belief system of worship.

Validity really has nothing to do with it anyway, since even some satanic black masses are valid.

In (Matthew 5:48), Christ said, *"You, therefore, must be perfect, as your heavenly Father is perfect."*

In (Matthew 22:39), Christ said, *"You shall love the Lord your God with all your heart, and with all your soul, and with all your mind. This is the great and first commandment."*

*"He that turneth away his ears from hearing the law, his prayer shall be an abomination."*(Book of Proverbs 28:9)

The Holy Sacrifice of the Mass is the greatest thing in Heaven and on earth!

The new mass is the abomination!

*"The Lord hateth all abomination of error, and they that fear him shall not love it."*(Ecclesiasticus 15:13)

*"Return to the Lord, and turn away from thy injustice, and greatly hate abomination."*(Ecclesiasticus 17:23)

## The Signs of the Times

*"32 And from the fig tree learn a parable: When the branch thereof is now tender, and the leaves come forth, you know that summer is nigh.*
*33 So you also, when you shall see all these things, know ye that it is nigh, even at the doors."*(Matt. 24)

This is the instruction of Christ.

Our Lord Jesus spoke, *"6 And you shall hear of wars and rumours of wars. See that ye be not troubled. For these things must come to pass, but the end is not yet.*
*7 For nation shall rise against nation, and kingdom against kingdom; and there shall be pestilences, and famines, and earthquakes in places:*
*8 Now all these are the beginnings of sorrows."*(Matt. 24)

The 20th century saw two world wars where nations and kingdoms rose up against each other.

The Cold War began and rumours of a Third World War have kept the world in a state of suspense.

The 20th century also witnessed some of the greatest pestilences, famines, and earthquakes ever recorded. Although Christ probably meant it in a symbolic nature such as heresies, schisms, etc. Both apply.

When these things take place, we are warned that the beginning of the end is now here.

*"30 And then shall appear the sign of the Son of man in heaven: and then shall all tribes of the earth mourn."*(Matt. 24)

In 1938, immediately before the great World War II, during what appeared to be a spectacular aurora borealis, a large white cross was formed in the sky as if being drawn slowly by a mystical hand. This event was witnessed by millions.

The lights were prophesied by Sister Lucia of Fatima as a warning that a war was about to erupt. Hitler himself saw the lights and believed it was sign for him to begin his conquest.

# Bird's Eye View of the Apocalypse

Adam and Eve desire to be like God and sin. Satan then has dominion over mankind (*the seven heads* which are ages of kings and *10 horns* which are the whole of nations of kings).

Adam's children again want to be like God and build the Tower of Babel and *the great city* only to be destroyed by God.

God establishes a covenant with Israel *(woman clothed with the sun)* as the People of God.

Rome (*the great city)* and its Empire *(woman/harlot)* gains most of the world of civilization.

Christ is born from Israel *(woman)* and establishes a New Covenant which includes all men to become the New Israel (*New Jerusalem)* known as His Church.

His death and resurrection destroys the power of Satan as he *(the Red Dragon)* is chained in Hell *(bottomless pit)* for *(a thousand years)* as the peace of Christ reigns in the hearts of Christians.

The spirit of antichrist *(mystery of iniquity)* united to men of the world is *(the first beast)*.

This beast attacks the Church *(woman clothed with the sun and taken into the wilderness)* with heresy, schism, and apostasy for *(1260 days,* symbolic number equaling the time Christ preached)*.

Heresies, schisms, and apostasies are the false religions which make-up *(the second beast)* also known as *(the false prophet)*.

This (*second beast makes*) the first beast (*worship*) himself.

The apostasy began within the Church throughout all the nations and specifically the church at Rome (*Babylon*).

Around the end of the symbolic 1260 days, church at Rome (*Babylon*) officially apostatizes and becomes part of the false prophet and the city becomes possessed (*the habitation of devils*).

(*After the 1000 years*), the angel (*restraining one*) loosens Satan (*the Red Dragon*) who then possesses the first beast which becomes (*scarlet*).

Antichrist (*scarlet beast*) is revealed through knowledge and application of advance sciences (*signs and wonders*).

The Faithful remnant of the church at Rome will (*come out of her*) since Christ said, *"My sheep hear my voice: and I know them, and they follow me."* (John 10:27)

Christ returns with a great (*fire*) that destroys antichrist and the false prophet sending them all to hell.

# The Key

God

New Heaven and New Earth = Heaven

Church (Triumphant in Heaven) = New Jerusalem

Seven Churches = Church (Militant on Earth) = New Jerusalem

Church = Old Israel/New Israel = Woman Clothed with the Sun

Satan = Red Dragon (7 heads, 10 horns) = Devil

7 = 1 or unity and perfection

10 = wholeness or completeness

Heads = ages or eras

Horns = kings = nations

Bottomless pit = Hell

Mystery of Iniquity = Spirit of antichrist

1st Beast = men of world with spirit of antichrist

2nd Beast = False Prophet = false religions

Babylon = Woman = Harlot = Roman Empire = church at Rome

Babylon fallen = Roman Empire destroyed = church at Rome apostatized

Scarlet Beast = 1st Beast Possessed = Antichrist

Abomination = New Mass (from apostate Roman Church)

# APPENDIX I

## Catholic Prophecies about the Apostasy

The following prophecies imply that Rome actually had the true Faith up until it loses it. This would necessarily mean that any religion contrary to Rome before it apostatizes would also mean that particular religion is not the true Faith, but rather a false religion, even satanic since it opposes the Church founded by Christ.

The purpose of giving these prophecies is to demonstrate that saints within the Church believed Rome will lose the Faith.

One may argue that some saints believed in a three days of darkness too but that doesn't mean it is true. Therefore, the prophecies of Rome losing the Faith don't necessarily mean they are true.

However, there is a major difference.

Cardinal Manning said that it was the *"universal testimony of the Fathers of the early Church"* that Rome will lose the Faith.

This is a far cry from saying that the three days of darkness was universally held.

Also, the Holy Scriptures are clear that a great apostasy shall happen.

This great apostasy implies that it can only be with the true Faith.

Therefore, since it is found in Holy Writ, and is the universal testimony of the Fathers, the weight of this teaching is quite heavy. It simply cannot be rejected as impossible or heretical.

## Henry Edward Cardinal Manning

*The Present Crisis of the Holy See*, 1861, London: Burns and Lambert, pp. 88-90

*"The apostasy of the city of Rome from the vicar of Christ and its destruction by Antichrist may be thoughts so new to many Catholics, that I think it well to recite the text of theologians of greatest repute. First Malvenda, who writes expressly on the subject, states as the opinion of Ribera, Gaspar Melus, Biegas, Suarrez, Bellarmine and Bosius that Rome shall apostatize from the faith, drive away the Vicar of Christ and return to its ancient paganism. ...Then the Church shall be scattered, driven into the wilderness, and shall be for a time, as it was in the beginning, invisible hidden in catacombs, in dens, in mountains, in lurking places; for a time it shall be swept, as it were from the face of the earth. Such is the universal testimony of the Fathers of the early Church."*

## St. Antony of the Desert (251-356):

*"Men will surrender to the spirit of the age. They will say that if they had lived in our day, Faith would be simple and easy. But in their day, they will say, things are complex; the Church must be brought up to date and made meaningful to the day's problems. When the Church and the World are one, then those days are at hand. Because our Divine Master placed a barrier between His things and the things of the world."* ([Disquisition CXIV] Quoted in *Voice of Fatima*, 23 January 1968)

The great St Athanasius wrote a biography on St Antony.

His life was filled with miracles, wisdom, and revelations. Satan and swarms of Devils attacked Antony on a regular basis.

He was nothing short of being one of the greatest saints who ever lived.

## St. Francis of Assisi

No introduction is needed for this great saint. St Bonaventure said Francis took Lucifer's place in Heaven when he died.

Shortly before he died, St. Francis of Assisi called together his followers and warned them of the coming troubles, saying:

*"1. The time is fast approaching in which there will be great trials and afflictions; perplexities and dissensions, both spiritual and temporal, will abound; the charity of many will grow cold, and the malice of the wicked will increase.*

*"2. The Devils will have unusual power, the immaculate purity of our Order, and of others, will be so much obscured that there will be very few Christians who will obey the true Sovereign Pontiff and the Roman Church with loyal hearts and perfect charity. At the time of this tribulation a man, not canonically elected, will be raised to the Pontificate, who, by his cunning, will endeavour to draw many into error and death.*

*"3. Then scandals will be multiplied, our Order will be divided, and many others will be entirely destroyed, because they will consent to error instead of opposing it.*

*"4. There will be such diversity of opinions and schisms among the people, the religious and the clergy, that, except those days were shortened, according to the words of the Gospel, even the elect would be led into error, were they not specially guided, amid such great confusion, by the immense mercy of God.*

"5. Then our Rule and manner of life will be violently opposed by some, and terrible trials will come upon us. Those who are found faithful will receive the crown of life; but woe to those who, trusting solely in their Order, shall fall into tepidity, for they will not be able to support the temptations permitted for the proving of the elect.

"6. Those who preserve their fervour and adhere to virtue with love and zeal for the truth, will suffer injuries and, persecutions as rebels and schismatics; for their persecutors, urged on by the evil spirits, will say they are rendering a great service to God by destroying such pestilent men from the face of the earth, but the Lord will be the refuge of the afflicted, and will save all who trust in Him. And in order to be like their Head, [Christ] these, the elect, will act with confidence, and by their death will purchase for themselves eternal life; choosing to obey God rather than man, they will fear nothing, and they will prefer to perish rather than consent to falsehood and perfidy.

"7. Some preachers will keep silence about the truth, and others will trample it under foot and deny it. Sanctity of life will be held in derision even by those who outwardly profess it, for in those days Jesus Christ will send them not a true Pastor, but a destroyer."

(Except for breaking up the narrative into numbered paragraphs and adding bold print for emphasis, the prophecy is presented without any alteration, as given in the *Works of the Seraphic Father St. Francis Of Assisi*, Washbourne, 1882, pp. 248-250)

Today, we see many completely at odds with the teachings of *The Syllabus of Errors* of Pope Pius IX and *Pascendi Dominici Gregis* (On the Doctrine of the Modernists) by Pope St. Pius X.

## St. Nicholas of Flue (1417-1487):

*"The Church will be punished because the majority of her members, high and low, will become so perverted. The Church will sink deeper and deeper until she will at last seem to be extinguished, and the succession of Peter and the other Apostles to have expired. But, after this, she will be victoriously exalted in the sight of all doubters."* (*Catholic Prophecy* by Yves Dupont, p. 30)

A short biography: St. Nicholas of Flue was born in Switzerland and later married to fill the desire of his pious parents. He and his wife, Dorothy had 10 children and was recognized by his neighbors as a very honorable and pious man and was chosen for public service. At 50 years of age, an interior voice said to him, *"Leave everything you love, and God will take care of you."* He had to undergo a distressing combat, but decided finally to leave everything — wife, children, house, lands — to serve God. After 25 years of marriage and public service, he kissed his wife and children goodbye, bade farewell to his neighbors and went into the forest to live as a hermit. He left, barefooted, clothed in a long grayish robe of coarse fabric, in his hand a rosary, without money or provisions, casting a final tender and prolonged gaze on his loved ones. His habitual prayer was this: *"My Lord and my God, remove from me all that can prevent me from going to You. My Lord and my God, give me all that can draw me to You."* One night God penetrated the hermit with a brilliant light, and from that time on he never again experienced hunger, thirst or cold. He settled in a nearby valley called Ranft where he tried to live in a hut of his own making, but the local people insisted upon building him a wooden cabin and a stone chapel. Distinguished persons came to him for counsel in matters of great importance. He lived for nineteen years only on the Holy Eucharist; the civil and ecclesiastical authorities, verified this fact as being beyond question.

The auxiliary bishop of Constance consecrated the chapel and even sent a priest to serve as Nicholas' private chaplain so he could attend Mass every day.

He saved Switzerland from civil war in 1480 with his wisdom. At the age of 70, Saint Nicholas fell ill with a very painful sickness which tormented him for eight days and nights without overcoming his patience. He was beatified in 1669 by Pope Clement IX, canonized in 1947, by Pope Pius XII.

## Our Lady of Good Fortune (Good Success)

*"...the Church will go through a dark night for lack of a Prelate and Father to watch over it..."*

Our Lady of Good Fortune appeared to Mother Mariana of Jesus Torres, in Quito, Ecuador, on February 2, 1634, with the child Jesus on her left arm and the scepter in her right hand. At her appearance the sanctuary light went out, which Our Lady stated had five meanings. Those having to do with the eclipse of the Church and the lack of a Pope in our century are:

*"First meaning: at the end of the 19th century and for a large part of the 20th, various heresies will flourish on this earth which will have become a free republic. The precious light of the Faith will go out in souls because of the almost total moral corruption: in those times there will be great physical and moral calamities, in private and in public. The little number of souls keeping the Faith and practicing the virtues will undergo cruel and unspeakable sufferings...*

*The third meaning of the lamp's going out is that in those times, the air will be filled with the spirit of impurity which like a deluge of filth will flood the streets, squares and public places. The licentiousness will be such that there will be no more virgin souls in the world.*

*A fourth meaning is that by having gained control of all the social classes, the sects will tend to penetrate with great skill into the heart of families and destroy even the children. The Devil will take glory in feeding perfidiously on the hearts of children. The innocence of childhood will almost disappear. Thus priestly vocations will be lost, it will be a real disaster. Priests will abandon their sacred duties and will depart from the path marked out for them by God. Then the Church will go through a dark night for lack of a Prelate and Father to watch over it with love, gentleness, strength and prudence, and numbers of priests will lose the spirit of God, thus placing their souls in great danger.*

*Pray constantly, cry out unwearyingly and weep unceasingly with bitter tears in the depths of your heart asking Our Father in Heaven, for love of the Eucharistic Heart of My Most Holy Son, for His Precious Blood, so generously shed for the profound bitterness and sufferings of His Passion and death, that He have pity on His ministers and that He put an end to such fatal times, by sending to His Church the Prelate who will restore the spirit of His priests.*

## La Salette

***"Rome will lose the faith and become the seat of the Antichrist... The Church will be in eclipse... At first, we will not know which is the true pope"***
(Words spoken by Our Lady of La Salette to Melanie Calvat in 1846 A.D., a fully approved Church Apparition, except this particular phrase)

(Abbot Combe: *"The Secret of Melanie and the Actual Crisis"*, Rome, 1906, p. 137) comments: *"For, in commenting on this part of the secret, Melanie said to the French Abbot Combe, "The Church will be eclipsed. At first, we will not know which is the true pope. Then secondly, the Holy Sacrifice of the Mass will cease to be offered in churches and houses; it will be such that, for a time, there will not be public services any more. But I see that the Holy Sacrifice has not really ceased: it will be offered in barns, in alcoves, in caves, and underground."*

There are two ways of interpreting this prophecy:

First: Rome is the temple of God thus the seat is the papacy.

Second: The temple is the universe and the antichrist will occupy all of it, even making the seat of Rome his own. In other words, the church at Rome will fall victim to the antichrist.

# Pope Leo XIII's Original Prayer to St. Michael

Pope Leo XIII's composition of the original Prayer to St. Michael the Archangel is one of the most fascinating and prophetic events in modern era.

On September 25, 1888, following his morning Mass, Pope Leo XIII fell into a trance leaving those in attendance thinking that he had just died. After coming to, Leo immediately went into his private chambers and composed the prayer to St. Michael. Afterwards, the Pope described what he had seen: a terrifying Vision of Christ and Satan speaking to each other over the tabernacle. The Devil told Jesus, *"I could destroy the Church and convert it to himself if he had more time and power over those who will give themselves to his service. Christ asked Satan, "How much time will you need?"* Satan said, *"75 to 100 years."* Our Lord, said, *"So be it, you will have the time and power"* and then the vision had vanished.

Pope Leo XIII commanded that his original Prayer to St. Michael the Archangel to be recited after all Low Mass as a protection for the Church against the attacks from Satan and his legions.

### The Original Prayer

### *The Raccolta,* 1930, Benzinger Bros., pp. 314-315.

*O Glorious Archangel St. Michael, Prince of the heavenly host, be our defense in the terrible warfare which we carry on against Principalities and Powers, against the rulers of this world of darkness, spirits of evil. Come to the aid of man, whom God created immortal, made in his own image and likeness, and redeemed at a great price from the tyranny of the Devil.*

*Fight this day the battle of the Lord, together with the holy angels, as already thou hast fought the leader of the proud angels, Lucifer, and his apostate host, who were powerless to resist thee, nor was there place for them any longer in Heaven.*

*That cruel, that ancient serpent, who is called the Devil or Satan, who seduces the whole world, was cast into the abyss with his angels. Behold, this primeval enemy and slayer of men has taken courage. Transformed into an angel of light, he wanders about with all the multitude of wicked spirits, invading the earth in order to blot out the name of God and of his Christ, to seize upon, slay and cast into eternal perdition souls destined for the crown of eternal glory. This wicked dragon pours out, as a most impure flood, the venom of his malice on men of depraved mind and corrupt heart, the spirit of lying, of impiety, of blasphemy, and the pestilent breath of impurity, and of every vice and iniquity.*

***These most crafty enemies have filled and inebriated with gall and bitterness the Church, the spouse of the immaculate Lamb, and have laid impious hands on her most sacred possessions. In the***

*Holy Place itself, where has been set up the See of the most holy Peter and the Chair of Truth for the light of the world, they have raised the throne of their abominable impiety, with the iniquitous design that when the Pastor has been struck, the sheep may be scattered.*

*Arise then, O invincible Prince, bring help against the attacks of the lost spirits to the people of God, and give them the victory. They venerate thee as their protector and Patron; in thee holy Church glories as her defense against the malicious power of hell; to thee has God entrusted the souls of men to be established in heavenly beatitude. Oh, pray to the God of peace that He may put Satan under our feet, so far conquered that he may no longer be able to hold men in captivity and harm the Church. Offer our prayers in the sight of the Most High, so that they may quickly conciliate the mercies of the Lord; and beating down the dragon, the ancient serpent, who is the Devil and Satan, do thou again make him captive in the abyss, that he may no longer seduce the nations. Amen*

*Behold the Cross of the Lord; be scattered ye hostile powers.*

*The Lion of the tribe of Judah has conquered, the root of David.*

*Let thy mercies be upon us, O Lord.*

*As we have hoped in thee.*

*O Lord, hear my prayer.*

*And let my cry come unto thee.*

*Let us pray.*

*O God, the Father of our Lord Jesus Christ, we call upon thy holy name, and as suppliants we implore thy clemency, that by the intercession of Mary, ever Virgin immaculate and our Mother, and of the glorious Archangel St. Michael, thou wouldst deign to help us against Satan and all other unclean spirits, who wander about the world for the injury of the human race and the ruin of souls. Amen.*

Notice the highlighted area. Pope Leo XIII knew how Satan was going to work out his plan. To raise the throne of the Satan's abominable impiety in the Holy Place (Rome) and to strike the shepherd (true Pope) would make the flock scatter. They also have laid their impious hands on the Church's most sacred possessions.

The Church's most sacred possessions are the Deposit of Faith (Scripture and Tradition). It was the Tradition of the Church, which was radically altered by the Vatican 2 sect, viz, the seven sacraments, and the Holy Mass.

It has been argued that Pope Leo was referring to his own day when composing this prayer as it coincides with the anti-Catholics trying to destroy the Church back then.

This may very well be the truth, but it also coincides with today's events.

In 1934, Pope Leo's prayer to St. Michael was changed to a shorter prayer which deleted the specific mention of Satan's plan; the very plan that Our Lady of La Salette, St. Francis of Assisi and St. Nicholas of Flue predicted.

However, John XXIII removed the prayer entirely from the Missal.

He also refused to announce the third secret of Fatima to the world as Our Lady asked.

# Fatima

### Exact words of Sister Lucia (visionary at Fatima) in an interview with Father Augustin Fuentes on December 26, 1957

*"Father, the Blessed Virgin is very sad because no one heeds her message; neither the good nor the bad. The good continue on with their life of virtue and apostolate, but they do not unite their lives to the message of Fatima. Sinners keep following the road of evil because they do not see the terrible chastisement about to befall them. Believe me, Father, God is going to punish the world and very soon. The chastisement of heaven is imminent. In less than two years, 1960 will be here and the chastisement of heaven will come and it will be very great. Tell souls to fear not only the material punishment that will befall us if we do not pray and do penance but most of all the souls who will go to hell."*

Sister Lucia clearly forewarned a chastisement would occur before 1960 and Our Lady is the one telling her this.

SEE APPENDIX 2   THE THIRD SECRET OF FATIMA

*"Sister Lucy also said to me: Father, we should not wait for an appeal to the world to come from Rome on the part of the Holy Father, to do penance. Nor should we wait for the call to penance to come from our bishops in our diocese, nor from the religious congregations. No! Our Lord has already very often used these means and the world has not paid attention. That is why now, it is necessary for each one of us to begin to reform himself spiritually. Each person must not only save his own soul but also all the souls that God has placed on our path ..."* *"The Devil does all in his power to distract us and to take away from us the love for prayer; we shall be saved together or we shall be damned together."*

*"Lucia found Jacinta sitting alone, still and very pensive, gazing at nothing. 'What are you thinking of, Jacinta?' 'Of the*

war that is going to come. So many people are going to die. And almost all of them are going to hell." (*Our Lady of Fatima*, p. 94; p. 92 in some versions)

Jacinta Marto (youngest visionary of Fatima) said almost all those who die in World War II will go to hell. Remember this is not even the Great Apostasy.

How much worse will it be?

Jacinta was found as an incorruptible when they disinterred her body in 1954. We should not take her words lightly.

## Pope Pius XII

*"We believe that the present hour is a dread phase of the events foretold by Christ. It seems that darkness is about to fall on the world. Humanity is in the grip of a supreme crisis."*

*"This persistence of Mary [at Fatima] about the dangers which menace the Church is a divine warning against the suicide of altering the Faith in her liturgy...In our [future] churches, Christians will search in vain or the red lamp where god awaits them."* (On the message of Our Lady of Fatima)

*"I hear all around me innovators who wish to dismantle the Sacred Chapel, destroy the universal flame of the Church, reject her ornaments and make her feel remorse for her historical past. A day will come when the civilized world will deny its God, when the Church will doubt as Peter doubted. She will be tempted to believe that man has become God. In our churches, Christians will search in vain for the red lamp where God awaits them. Like Mary Magdalene, weeping before the empty tomb they will ask, "Where have they taken Him?"* (Cardinal Eugenio Pacelli, later Pope Pius XII, to Count Enrico P. Galeazzi)

It has been reported that Pope Pius XII spoke the following:

*"After me the deluge."*

If he indeed made this statement, then we have a clear referencing of (Matt. 24, Luke 17, and I Peter 3.)

# APPENDIX II

## The Third Secret of Fatima

Sister Maria das Dores (Lucia de Santos), the oldest seer, once told Father Augustin Fuentes on December 26, 1957, *"Father, the Blessed Virgin is very sad because no one heeds her message; neither the good nor the bad. The good continue on with their life of virtue and apostolate, but they do not unite their lives to the message of Fatima. Sinners keep following the road of evil because they do not see the terrible chastisement about to befall them. Believe me, Father, God is going to punish the world and very soon. The chastisement of heaven is imminent. In less than two years, 1960 will be here and the chastisement of heaven will come and it will be very great. Tell souls to fear not only the*

*material punishment that will befall us if we do not pray and do penance but most of all the souls who will go to hell."*(1)

She clearly forewarned of a very great chastisement and it would occur within the next two years.

So what was it? What very great chastisement befell the world between the years 1958 and 1960?

Was Sister Lucia a false prophet?

**Sister Lucia at approximately 40 years of age**

Lucia from Our Lady clearly prophesied the Spanish Civil War under Pope Pius XI and World War II under Pope Pius XII which the world experienced just 13 years earlier.

Are we not to suppose that a greater chastisement will befall the world?

The Third Secret, written down by Sister Lucia in 1939, was given to the popes down though the years and was supposed to be revealed by the pope in 1960 or after Sister Lucia's death, which ever happened first, because the world would better understand its contents in that time period. (2)

The Third Secret was not revealed in and by 1960.

Our Lady must have known that Lucia would die around 1960 or else there would be no reason for Our Lady to make such a request.

Yet, the request almost implies that Lucia would die without the world knowing about it since a year was also given.

All this is very interesting because, without a doubt, pictures of the Lucia before 1960 show a different person than the Lucia after that year.

The fact that she was silenced yet had publically contradicted herself several times with public photos that were completely out of character, one would either have to conclude that a massive cover-up was hand or the whole Fatima story is simply a fraud.

**A young and happy Sister Lucia**

Since Our Lady foreknew the chastisements of the wars in the 1930's and 1940's, then by logical deduction, Our Lady foresaw that her Third Secret would not be revealed in 1960.

By implication, our Lady was attempting to tell us something about the chastisement which would have already begun by 1960.

When one claiming to be pope refused to reveal the secret, our Lady was giving us the dynamics of her secret with Rome's omission.

In hindsight, the chastisement must have been about the Church and the papacy.

## Father Malachi Martin

Malachi Martin sees sinister workings in the Church.

The late Fr. Malachi Martin, doctor, exorcist, linguist, and advisor to several *"popes,"* and made secret cardinal and bishop by Pope Pius XII, read the Third Secret in 1960 along with Cardinal Bea and John XXIII.

According Fr. Malachi Malachi, John XXIII did not believe in Fatima and therefore refused to read the Secret because it was not in line with what John XXIII had in mind for the future of the Church. (3) In 1962, at the Second Vatican Council, John XXIII referred to the three seers of Fatima as *"Prophets of Doom."* (4) This is interesting since John XXIII called Fatima, *"the center of all Christian hopes."* (5) Yet, he refused to read the Third Secret in 1960.

Fr. Malachi Martin gave clues to the Third Secret saying the Secret was far worse than even a nuclear war. It would fill confessionals and Churches and it did not involve the chastisements as the earlier wars. (6)

Before Fr. Malachi Martin died, he actually revealed the Third Secret to close friends and began a tell-all book on the New Vatican. Part of that secret was about the appearance of Antichrist. With great sadness, Fr. Malachi came to hold the sede vacant position after visiting Rome and being told by John Paul II that his faith was not the same. Part of the secret was the appearance of the final antichrist. (7)

**Father Malachi left the Jesuit order and ceased to be a member of the clergy (why he is pictured without the Roman collar), however, he remained a practicing priest saying his daily masses and hearing confessions.**

Eleven months after the death of Fr. Malachi Martin, Rome reveals what they say is the contents of the Third Secret, claiming it was about John Paul II and the attempt on his life in 1981. (8)

Since the world was told that it would better understand the meaning of the Third Secret in 1960, we know that what Rome revealed in 2000 and their conclusion was a complete fabrication concocted to deflect the real Secret and its meaning.

Not only that but what modernist Rome revealed was not shocking, would not fill any confessional as it didn't, nor would there be any reason for John XXIII not to reveal what Rome actually revealed 40 years later. Not to mention the fact that it was conveniently revealed after the death of Fr. Malachi Martin, the one man who could have and would have refuted their lie.

A great apostasy is the only thing worse than any war. An apostasy can only happen with the falling away from the true Faith.

The 1958 conclave elects a known modernist and Mason who, in turn, immediately revises the mass and calls a Council when there was absolutely no need in doing so. The Church was booming with converts, priest, religious, and lay people.

That the papacy has been usurped and the true faith was replaced by a counterfeit version with millions of Catholics being led astray from Truth right into hell was no doubt this great chastisement warned of the late Lucia.

The whole message of Fatima was about saving souls from hell.

The Third Secret did not specifically say anything about the conclave or an election of some antipope or Fr. Malachi Martin would have become a sedevacantist immediately but rather it indicated an apostasy from the top and the coming antichrist, which would initiate the great apostasy.

A true pope would not try to usurp the authority of Heaven and this is precisely what John XXIII did after calling it the center of all Christian hopes.

The truly faithful believe in Fatima because they know the miracles that have come from it could not possibly come from hell or else the Catholic Church already defected by approving it. Remember, the Church was fully aware of the contents of the Secret when She approved the apparition.

Pope Pius XII did fulfill our Lady's promise when he consecrated specifically Russia to the Immaculate Heart of Mary on July 7, 1952. She never promised he would do it with all the bishops but that he would do it none-the-less. (9)

Consequently, Russia converted out of its Communist ways ending the persecution on her Christians and there was a certain period of peace. The nations that were annihilated into the Soviet Union have regained their sovereignty. (10)

(1.) Controversy has surrounded this interview with Fr. Augustin Fuentes. Two years later, an anonymous note came from the episcopal curia of Coimbra denouncing the interview as fraudulent. Sr. Lucy was then silenced. Fr. Joaquin Alonso, who wrote over 5,000 documents on Fatima at the request of the bishop of Fatima, wrote in 1975 that the interview with Fr. Augustine Fuentes was authentic.

(2.) *Our Lady of Fatima*, MacMillion, First Edition 1947, p. 211, by William Thomas Walsh, and Sermon, Third Secret of Fatima, Most Reverend Robert F. McKenna O.P.

(3.) Coast to Coast AM radio program, May 8, 1998, Art Bell with Fr. Malachi Martin

(4.) Fr. Malachi Martin referred to the opening speech at the Second Vatican Council in the 1998 interview with Art Bell

(5.) *Fatima, The Great Sign,* Tan, p. 12, by Francis Johnston

(6.) Coast to Coast AM radio program, May 8, 1998, Art Bell with Fr Malachi Martin

(7.) Private exchanges with his closest friends.

(8.) *Inside the Vatican,* Special Supplement June-July 2000, and *Inside the Vatican* June-July 2000

(9.) *Fatima, The Great Sign,* Tan, p. 89, by Francis Johnston, states that Lucia wrote after the 1952 Consecration of Russia, *"I am grieved that it has not yet been carried out as Our Lady had asked. Patience! ... Let us hope that Our Lady, as a good Mother, will be pleased to accept it."* The initial quote in 1917 stated by Our Lady, *"In the end, ...The Holy Father will consecrate Russia to me; it will be converted."*

(10.) *Our Lady of Fatima,* MacMillion, First Edition 1947, p. 226, by William Thomas Walsh, indicates the conversion of Russia referred by Our Lady was conversion out of Communism since this is the error that needed to be corrected by the papal consecration before it spreads to every nation.

# Index of Biblical Citations

| Genesis | Pages |
|---|---|
| 3:15 | 7, 105 |
| 3:3-6 | 53 |
| 5:4 | 31 |
| 11:3-5 | 53 |
| 17:14 | 41 |

| Exodus | |
|---|---|
| 12:15-19 | 41 |
| 20:3-5 | 113 |
| 30:33-38 | 41 |
| 31:14 | 41 |

| Leviticus | |
|---|---|
| 7:20-27 | 41 |
| 17:4-14 | 41 |
| 18:29 | 41 |
| 19:8 | 41 |
| 20:17-18 | 41 |
| 22:3 | 41 |

| | |
|---|---|
| 23:29 | 41 |

**Numbers**

| | |
|---|---|
| 9:13 | 41 |
| 15:30-31 | 41 |
| 19:13-20 | 41 |

**1 Kings (3 Kings)**

| | |
|---|---|
| 10:14 | 112 |

**Psalms**

| | |
|---|---|
| 37 | 41 |
| 95 | 91, 92 |

**Proverbs**

| | |
|---|---|
| 3:32 | 133 |
| 12:22 | 138 |
| 15:9 | 138 |
| 15:26 | 129 |
| 28:9 | 150 |

**Sirach (Ecclesiasticus)**

| | |
|---|---|
| 15:13 | 150 |
| 17:23 | 150 |

| | |
|---|---|
| 44:16 | 31 |
| 49:14 | 31 |

**Isaiah (Isaias)**

| | |
|---|---|
| 61:1-3 | 40 |

**Jeremiah (Jeremias)**

| | |
|---|---|
| 44:7-11 | 41 |
| 51:6 | 41 |

**Ezekiel (Ezechiel)**

| | |
|---|---|
| 21:3-4 | 41 |

**Daniel**

| | |
|---|---|
| 4:14 | 41 |
| 8:20 | 108 |
| 9:26 | 41 |
| 12:11-112 | 107 |

**Hosea (Osee)**

| | |
|---|---|
| 3:4 | 40, 45 |

**Amos**

| | |
|---|---|
| 9:14 | 40 |

**Malachi (Malachias)**

4:4-5           29

## 1 Maccabees (1 Machabees)

1:20-43       129  
1:44-53       130  
1:54-59       131  

## 2 Maccabees (2 Machabees)

6:4            127, 131, 149

# NEW TESTAMENT

## The Holy Gospel of Jesus Christ, according to St. Matthew

| | |
|---|---|
| 5:48 | 150 |
| 7:15 | 43 |
| 7:15-16 | 97 |
| 10:16-18 | 22 |
| 10:22 | 22 |
| 11:5 | 40 |
| 11:10-15 | 32 |
| 12:18 | 40 |
| 15:4 | 43 |
| 17:10-13 | 32 |
| 18:6 | 120 |
| 19:20-23 | 113 |
| 22:39 | 150 |
| 24: | 17, 45 |
| 24:3 | 11 |
| 24:4 | 43 |
| 24:6-8 | 151 |
| 24:11 | 100 |
| 24:12 | 22 |
| 24:13 | 108 |
| 24:14 | 11, 40 |
| 24:15 | 149 |
| 24:16-21 | 119 |

| | |
|---|---|
| 24:21 | 44 |
| 24:19-31 | 21 |
| 24:24 | 43, 101, 105, 110 |
| 24:25 | 101 |
| 24:30 | 11, 151 |
| 24:32-33 | 151 |
| 24:34 | 17 |
| 24:35 | 120 |
| 24:38-39 | 44 |
| 24:40-41 | 19, 20 |
| 24:44 | 100 |
| 25:13 | 100 |
| 26:28 | 146, 147 |

## The Holy Gospel of Jesus Christ, according to St. Mark

| | |
|---|---|
| 9:42 | 120 |
| 12:29-31 | 84 |
| 13:10 | 11, 40 |
| 13:19 | 44 |
| 13:22 | 110 |
| 13:24-27 | 21 |
| 14:24 | 146, 147 |
| 14:26 | 11 |

## The Holy Gospel of Jesus Christ, according to St. Luke

| | |
|---|---|
| 1:13-17 | 33 |
| 4:18-21 | 40 |
| 11:23 | 109 |

| | |
|---|---|
| 12:40 | 100 |
| 17:2 | 120 |
| 17:26 | 30 |
| 17:34-35 | 23 |
| 18:8 | 45 |

## The Holy Gospel of Jesus Christ, according to St. John

| | |
|---|---|
| 8: | 90 |
| 10:27 | 154 |
| 11:24 | 21 |
| 14:27 | 23 |
| 15:19 | 109 |
| 16:33 | 24 |
| 17:12 | 101 |

## Acts of the Apostles

| | |
|---|---|
| 1:11 | 21 |
| 2:16-22 | 15 |
| 5:15 | 111 |
| 5:29-31 | 40, 41 |
| 12:2 | 34 |
| 15:14-18 | 40 |
| 20:29-31 | 43 |

## Epistle of St. Paul the Apostle to the Romans

| | |
|---|---|
| 6:4 | 42 |
| 9:28 | 38 |
| 11:20-29 | 37 |
| 11:24 | 38 |
| 11:25 | 38, 39 |
| 11:26 | 39 |
| 11:27 | 40 |
| 11:28 | 39 |
| 16:17 | 43 |

## First Epistle of St. Paul to the Corinthians

| | |
|---|---|
| 7:31 | 121 |
| 10:20 | 92 |
| 11:1-12 | 95 |
| 11:1-16 | 96 |
| 11:29 | 147 |
| 14:33-38 | 96 |

## Second Epistle of St. Paul to the Corinthians

| | |
|---|---|
| 11:3 | 43 |
| 13: | 43 |

## Epistle of St. Paul to the Galatians

| | |
|---|---|
| 1:6-9 | 43 |
| 1:8 | 91 |

### Epistle of St. Paul to the Ephesians

| | |
|---|---|
| 2:19 | 24 |
| 4:14 | 43 |
| 5: | 34 |
| 5:22-33 | 96 |
| 5:31-32 | 24 |

### Epistle of St. Paul to the Philippians

| | |
|---|---|
| 3:2 | 43 |
| 3:3 | 41 |
| 3:18 | 43 |

### Epistle of St. Paul to the Colossians

| | |
|---|---|
| 2:8-18 | 43 |
| 2:11 | 42 |
| 3:4 | 11 |
| 3:18 | 46 |

### First Epistle of St. Paul to the Thessalonians

| | |
|---|---|
| 4: | 21 |
| 4:13-17 | 19 |
| 4:1-17 | 20 |

### Second Epistle of St. Paul to the Thessalonians

| | |
|---|---|
| 2: | 17, 45, 50 |
| 2:3 | 11, 43, 11 |
| 2:3-11 | 45, 99 |
| 2:6 | 105 |
| 2:7-8 | 11, 19, 21, 101 |

| | |
|---|---|
| 2:9-10 | 101 |
| 2:15 | 12, 20, 6 |

## First Epistle of St. Paul to Timothy

| | |
|---|---|
| 1:10 | 43 |
| 2:11-15 | 96 |
| 6:9-10 | 112, 113 |
| 6:14 | 11 |

## Second Epistle of St. Paul to Timothy

| | |
|---|---|
| 1:10 | 11 |
| 2:7 | 43 |
| 4:1 | 11 |
| 4:8 | 11 |
| 4:3-4 | 16, 45 |

## Epistle of St. Paul to Titus

| | |
|---|---|
| 2:5 | 96 |
| 2:13 | 11 |

## Epistle of St. Paul to the Hebrews

| | |
|---|---|
| 1: | 16 |
| 3:12 | 44 |
| 6:4-8 | 44 |
| 9:28 | 11 |
| 10:16 | 41 |

| | |
|---|---|
| 10:26-29 | 44 |
| 11:3 | 31 |
| 11:32-40 | 22 |
| 12:1-13 | 22 |
| 12:24-29 | 44 |
| 13:9 | 44 |
| 13:10 | 41 |

## Catholic Epistle of St. James the Apostle

| | |
|---|---|
| 5:17 | 31 |

## First Epistle of St. Peter the Apostle

| | |
|---|---|
| 1:3-9 | 22 |
| 1:20 | 20 |
| 2:18-25 | 20 |
| 3:8 | 23 |
| 3:13-17 | 20 |
| 4:1 | 20 |
| 4:17 | 24 |
| 5:4 | 100 |
| 5:8 | 100 |
| 5:13 | 101 |

## Second Epistle of St. Peter the Apostle

| | |
|---|---|
| 2:1 | 22 |
| 3:3-8 | 16 |

| | |
|---|---|
| 3:10 | 121 |
| 3:16 | 20 |

## First Epistle of St. John the Apostle

| | |
|---|---|
| 2:18 | 16, 99 |
| 2:22 | 99 |
| 2:28 | 11, 34 |
| 3:2 | 11 |
| 3:7-8 | 44 |
| 4:1-3 | 44, 99 |

## Second Epistle of St. John the Apostle

| | |
|---|---|
| 7:7 | 99 |
| 7-11 | 44 |

## Third Epistle of St. John the Apostle

| | |
|---|---|
| 9: | 43 |

## Apocalypse of St. John the Apostle

| | |
|---|---|
| 2: | 117 |
| 2:9 | 104 |
| 3:9 | 104 |
| 3:12 | 39 |
| 11:1-19 | 29, 30 |
| 11:3 | 107 |
| 11:7 | 103 |
| 12: | 103 |
| 12:3 | 115 |
| 12:6-8 | 102, 107 |

| | |
|---|---|
| 12:12 | 107 |
| 13:1 | 103 |
| 13:2 | 104 |
| 13:4 | 105 |
| 13:5 | 106 |
| 13:11 | 108 |
| 13:12 | 108 |
| 13:13-15 | 105, 111 |
| 13:14-17 | 111 |
| 13:18 | 112 |
| 14:9-11 | 112 |
| 16:2 | 109 |
| 16:10 | 109 |
| 16:13 | 108 |
| 17: | 45 |
| 17:3 | 113 |
| 17:4-8 | 114 |
| 17:9 | 116 |
| 17:9-12 | 115 |
| 17:13-16 | 116 |
| 17:15 | 104 |
| 17:17-18 | 117 |
| 18: | 45 |
| 18:1-2 | 117 |
| 18:3-4 | 118 |
| 18:7-9 | 119 |
| 18:10 | 120 |
| 18:21-22 | 120 |
| 18:23 | 121 |
| 19:7-16 | 11 |
| 19:20 | 108 |

| | |
|---|---|
| 20:3-4 | 105, 107 |
| 20:5-6 | 26 |
| 20:7 | 26 |
| 20:10 | 108 |
| 20:11-13 | 11 |
| 21:1-2 | 26 |

www.ingramcontent.com/pod-product-compliance
Lightning Source LLC
Chambersburg PA
CBHW021921180426
**43200CB00027B/176**